memories in miniature

creating small photo gifts and keepsakes that make BIG impressions

Pamela Frye Hauer

MEMORY
MAKERS
BOOKS

Managing Editor MaryJo Regier
Author and Artist Pamela Frye Hauer
Editor Emily Curry Hitchingham
Art Director Nick Nyffeler
Graphic Designers Jordan Kinney, Robin Rozum
Art Acquisitions Editor Janetta Abucejo Wieneke
Craft Editor Jodi Amidei
Photographer Ken Trujillo
Contributing Photographers Brenda Martinez, Jennifer Reeves
Editorial Support Karen Cain, Amy Glander, MaryJo Regier, Dena Twinem
Hand model Emily Curry Hitchingham

Memory Makers® Memories in Miniature

Published by Memory Makers Books, an imprint of F+W Publications, Inc.

12365 Huron Street, Suite 500, Denver, CO 80234

Phone (800) 254-9124

First edition. Printed in the United States.

09 08 07 06 05 5 4 3 2 1

Library of Congress Cataloging-in-Publication Data

Hauer, Pamela Frye.
    Memories in miniature : creating small photo gifts and keepsakes that make big
impressions / Pamela Frye Hauer.
        p. cm.
    Includes bibliographical references and index.
    ISBN 1-892127-50-4
    1. Photograph albums. 2. Photographs--Conservation and restoration. 3. Scrapbooks. 4.
Miniature craft. I. Title

TR465.H38 2005
745.5--dc22

                                                                2005043854

Distributed to trade and art markets by
F+W Publications, Inc.
4700 East Galbraith Road, Cincinnati, OH 45236
Phone (800) 289-0963
ISBN 1-892127-50-4

Distributed in Canada by Fraser Direct
100 Armstrong Avenue
Georgetown, ON, Canada L7G 5S4
Tel: (905) 877-4411

Distributed in the U.K. and Europe by David & Charles
Brunel House, Newton Abbot, Devon, TQ12 4PU, England
Tel: (+44) 1626 323200, Fax: (+44) 1626 323319
E-mail: mail@davidandcharles.co.uk

Distributed in Australia by Capricorn Link
P.O. Box 704, S. Windsor NSW, 2756 Australia
Tel: (02) 4577-3555

Memory Makers Books is the home of Memory Makers, the scrapbook magazine dedicated to educating and inspiring scrapbookers.
To subscribe, or for more information, call (800) 366-6465.
Visit us on the Internet at www.memorymakersmagazine.com.

For Milton

Table of Contents

Ok, I'll admit it. I'm a pack rat! I like to collect things. . .lots of things, especially photos and souvenirs of the past. Starting with the piles of photos and stacks of keepsakes my parents saved, I continued the family tradition with my own camera and collections at a very young age. Sometimes I wonder if I save too much, but every time I throw something out, I end up wanting it later on for one reason or another. Regardless of whether I'm working on an art or craft project, a gift, or a scrapbook page, I always end up pulling out my boxes and albums to find materials that end up providing the perfect final touch.

Whether you're as avid a "collector" as I am, or simply like taking a few precious photos of important events, we all could use an easy way to keep these items organized and documented that allow us to show them off at the same time.

The projects in *Memories in Miniature* show you how to do just that: to turn your photos and other mementos into wonderful keepsakes, meaningful gifts and greetings, home décor and more. Because they are small in size, all of the projects are relatively quick and simple but will definitely stir up big memories and reactions while helping you manage and make use of your own collections and mementos. Using the featured projects as your foundation, you can customize the decorations and embellishments for each as simply or ornately as you would like for any style or occasion.

I'm sure you'll find many fun ideas in this book to try, whether you're an artist in the making or an avid crafter or scrapbooker. So get set to put your imagination to work to turn your memories into mementos that are small in size but not in meaning!

Pamela

Pamela Frye Hauer

Artist and Author

TOOLS

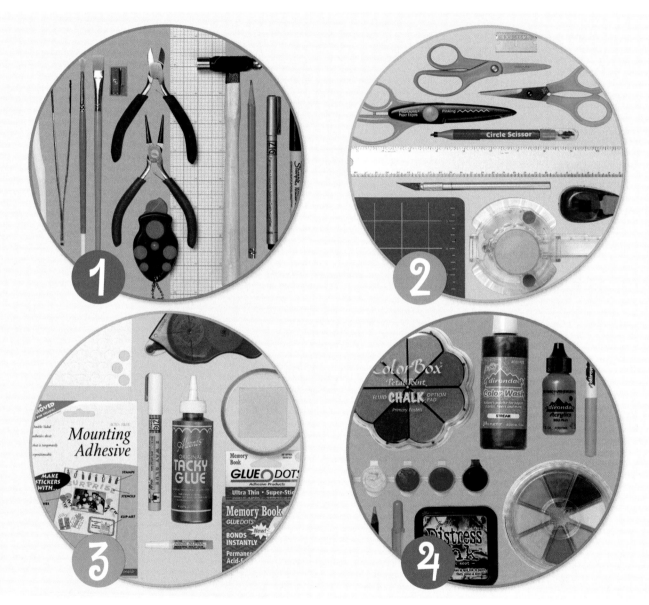

1 Basic

The basic tools you'll need for creating the projects in this book: bone folder, tweezers, paintbrushes, pencil sharpener, wire cutters, needle-nose pliers, scoring tool, clear grid ruler, small hammer, pencil, pen and permanent marker.

2 Cutting

Options for cutting different types of materials and for cutting in different patterns or shapes: utility blade, small scissors, decorative edged scissors, circle scissors, metal ruler, craft knife and sharp blades, cutting mat, circle cutter and paper punches.

3 Bonding

The primary kinds of adhesives you'll find handy for different types of materials and situations: dimensional adhesive, dry adhesive applicator, double-sided sheet adhesive, glue pen, wet glue, super-strength glue, double-sided tape, adhesive pickup square and adhesive dots.

4 Coloring

Pick your favorites for coloring and decorating your creations: ink pads, color wash, dimensional paint writers, multisurface ink pens, acrylic paints, colored pencils, markers, distressing ink and chalks.

Besides your camera, the two main tools you'll need to create the projects in this book are a cutting implement and archival-quality adhesives. Many of the cutting techniques can be performed with your choice of a small pair of scissors or a sharp craft knife, depending on what you are most comfortable with. If one should be used over the other for better results, it will be listed in the materials list for each project. For cleanest cuts and for safety's sake, always use a metal-edged ruler in place of the plastic variety when cutting straight lines with a craft knife. Depending on the kind of materials you will be adhering to your project, you'll find a couple of forms of adhesives particularly handy. "Dry adhesives" such as double-sided tapes, tabs and sheets work best for adhering paper and other flat, lightweight items. "Wet adhesives" such as liquid glue and adhesive dots are designed to adhere heavier dimensional items.

Additionally, there are a few basic tools shown here that will be of use on most projects as well as many optional tools, depending upon the specific project and type of adornments. Again, any specific items that you will need will be listed in the supplies list for each project. A few tools not pictured include a home computer, scanner and printer. These are suggested for select projects, but are not necessary as the services of a professional copy shop provide an inexpensive alternative. Other tools you could utilize that are not pictured include templates, sewing machines, die-cutting machines and others, depending on what you already own and prefer to use.

5 Stamping

A quick and attractive way to add patterns, accents and lettering to your projects: clear embossing pad; solvent ink; colored embossing powders and various pattern, design, saying and alphabet rubber stamps.

6 Coating

For sealing and protecting the surface of projects, especially those that will be frequently handled: paper glaze, de-acidifying spray, paper glitter and glitz, clear embossing powder and decoupage medium.

7 Binding

The types of tools you can use to help bind your own small books and albums: needle and thread, hand drill, eyelet setter, push pin, hole punch, binding punch and discs, stapler and foam pad.

8 And More

Some optional tools you may find helpful: heat tool, label maker, funnel, cleanup tray, ink applicator, engraver and dimensional appliqué.

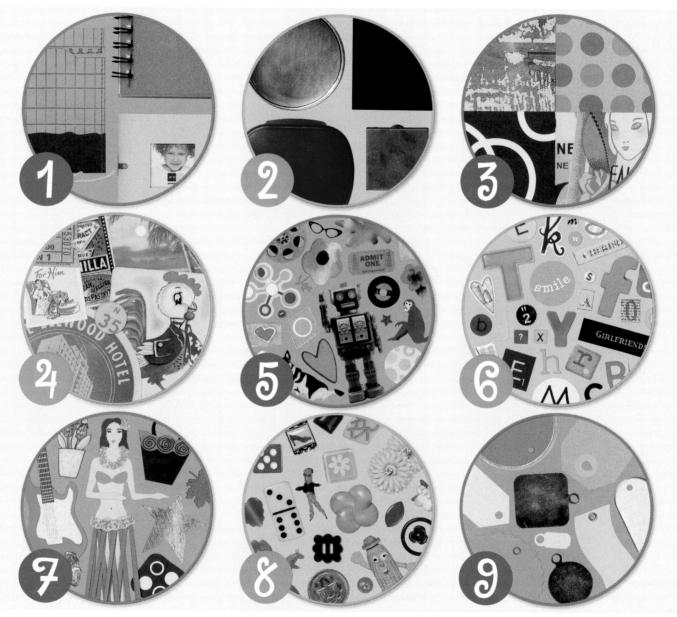

1 Albums
Pick from the many mini books on the market, or build your own out of paper or other materials.

2 Containers
Small organizational items or clean candy containers provide the perfect size.

3 Papers
There are limitless types and prints to choose from, or you can create your own patterns with stamps, inks, paints and pencils.

4 Ephemera
Use new, vintage or reproduction labels, cards, tickets and the like.

5 Stickers
Who doesn't love to use these quick, clean and easy decorations?

6 Lettering
Use stickers, alphabet stamps or dimensional letters for great options. You can also print wording with a computer or add journaling the "old-fashioned" way—by hand with a pen.

7 Die Cuts
There are many unique pre-cut designs, or you can invest in a die-cutting machine and dies for custom creations.

8 3D Accents
Purchase small embellishments sold for scrapbooking and crafts, or raid your jewelry box and junk drawer for more fun items.

9 Tags
Great for decorating accents, for adding journaling to your project, or as the pages of a bound mini album.

The most important parts of your mini memory crafts are, of course, your photos and mementos. But beyond those exist almost limitless materials with which you may choose to present and decorate your memories. Pick a foundation for your project such as a small album or container, or even choose something unusual like a snow dome. Next, decide on the colors and style you'd like your piece to be, making sure to remember to find lettering that will work for your titles and journaling. To dress and decorate your piece, search your existing stash of supplies and collections or go shopping for new accents and embellishments.

Memories in Miniature is filled with fun ideas for adorning your projects, but you should feel free to design and accent your projects in any style you'd like. Also keep in mind that you can finish a project quickly by using alphabet stickers and minimal embellishments. Alternatively, if time allows you can handcut your own letters from paper and add more intricate accents such as bead work. Each potential material simply could not be listed here, and select items such as wooden craft shapes and acrylic squares will be listed in the materials lists as necessary. With so many items presented for you, use as few or as many as you'd like to personalize your own mini memory masterpieces.

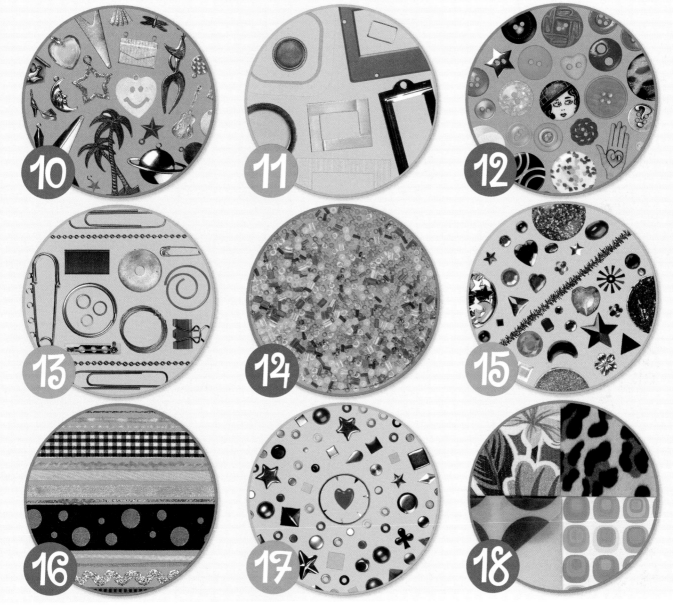

10 Charms
Choose from a multitude of varieties available to find the perfect image for accenting your piece.

11 Frames
Bind them together to make a mini book or use them to accentuate an important part of your project.

12 Buttons
A simple and classic decoration for crafts of all kinds.

13 Findings
Search through office, hardware and jewelry-making supplies to find great binding materials and more.

14 Beads
String them on wire for a handle, glue them on as tiny accents or cover an entire surface with colorful beads.

15 Glitz
Make your project shine and sparkle with glitter, tinsel, rhinestones, sequins or mini mirrors.

16 Fibers
Strings and ribbons of any width are a beautiful way to bind or decorate many projects.

17 Metals
Bind or adorn your piece with brads, eyelets, nailheads or studs.

18 And More
Oilcloth, fabric, envelopes, stationery, transparencies and many other materials can be incorporated!

Keeping Memories

Include photos and mementos to create quick little albums about tropical trips, a best friend or any subject you can think of!

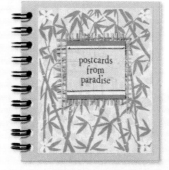

Gifts

Handmade albums, books and journals make meaningful, personalized presents for anyone and for any occasion. Add photos of your co-worker for an original retirement gift, or decorate a wearable journal with pictures and quotes to give to a dear friend or family member.

Greetings & Invitations

Mini books make unique birthday, holiday, thank-you cards and invitations worthy of saving. Include information on each page of mini album invitations and be sure to enclose them in mini envelopes. For a thank-you book, include photos from a visit with friends, or photos of the gift being used.

Party Favors & Announcements

Print wording with your computer and use stickers for fast means of decorating a number of identical pieces. For a dinner party with old friends, find shots of them from high school for a fun and funny favor, or announce an engagement or birth with shaped tags bound with a brad.

Your memories are larger than life, so why preserve and present them in such a mini manner? There are many reasons, the primary one being they're just so cute! Who can resist mini versions of their favorite products and foods? Small size alone turns common, everyday objects into fun and funky novelties. Likewise, scaled down keepsakes transform cherished memories into pieces of art that are not only compact and portable, but that are just as meaningful as their larger counterparts. In addition to little books and albums, there are several other ideas for memory crafts that just happen to be on the small side, such as magnets and jewelry. If you're a scrapbooker, these mini mementos make great additions to your library of full-sized albums. You can create reduced-size versions of your larger pieces to give as gifts, favors or to use as "brag books" showcasing your work. Small-scale keepsakes are also ideal for featuring topics and events that just don't fit the themes of your regular albums. Moreover, many of the mini projects in this book can be added directly onto your regular scrapbook pages. Ultimately, mini projects are a fun and unique means of preserving and presenting your memories—but their uses and benefits don't end there. Look to the list below for even more ideas for potential miniature projects.

Managing Mementos

Go through those piles of keepsakes and turn them into cute little time capsules. Organize airplane, concert, movie or sports tickets chronologically and incorporate photos and info about who was there and why.

Record Keeping

Take useful information and make it accessible and attractive at the same time. Make an album featuring the make and model of past cars you have owned, or make an album with your current or past job positions or home projects. Don't forget the photos!

Show & Tell

Make mini "brag books" that can be carried with you anytime to flaunt photos of your home, your grandchildren or a prized collection. To make an album that fits perfectly in a purse, make reduced-size copies of your favorite full-sized scrapbook pages and place them in a little handmade book that closes with a ribbon.

Organizing

Find and decorate fun containers, boxes and tins to organize and safely contain your compact creations, making sure they aren't made of materials that will deteriorate and damage your albums over time.

MANY MINI OPTIONS!

Scrapbooking Supplies

There are thousands of variations of albums, papers, die cuts, stickers, stamps and embellishments, and new lines of each are constantly being added to the market. Stamp and emboss a sun for a simple album cover, use a colored chain to connect a mini tag album or use metal clips to bind tiny file folders.

Art & Craft Supplies

Look for blank sketchbooks, interesting journals and a multitude of colorants and coatings for your projects at art supply stores. Check out craft stores for cardboard and wooden shapes and boxes as well as many, many more ideas. Decorate a sketchbook cover for a Christmas album, or paint and adorn a small box with photos and belongings of a beloved relative.

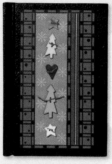

Office Supplies

Select from traditional styles or more contemporary designs of mailing labels, address books, sticky notes, paper clips and much more. Use alphabetical file cards to create a small school album or place little pages inside a plastic business card holder.

Hardware & Home-Improvement Supplies

Buy metal tags, key tags and bead chain and save paint and laminate chips from your own home do-it-yourself project. Use the paint chips you chose when decorating a nursery to create an accordion book featuring the final decor, or attach metal-rimmed tags together for a small keepsake of a relative.

Besides the numerous blank books and albums available at scrapbooking, craft and art stores, there are many other options for the "base" of mini memory crafts. Several companies sell kits for making little albums out of any paper you choose, and there are dozens of ways to bind books of your own creation. Search your home and stores for many materials besides craft paper that can be used, such as bingo cards, postcards, cloth, business cards, index cards—almost anything! Moreover, your mini memory crafts aren't limited to books and albums. Display your favorite photos in small shadow boxes, frames, tins, or as jewelry, magnets, coasters or key chains. Below are several sources for getting started, but the options are limited only by your imagination!

Cards & Stationery

While on shopping trips, keep an eye out for attractive notepads, notecards and stationery sets to adorn with your own titles and photos. Add a title and photos to a pretty purse notepad, embellish and fill a decorative envelope or fill a diary with facts about your family heritage.

Found & Vintage Items

Collect cool pamphlets, books and packaging from yard sales, antique stores and thrift shops to create one-of-a-kind mini memory crafts.

Home Accessories

Add extra adornments to small home décor items for an impressive display or to present as customized gifts. Decorate little frames, candleholders, paperweights, clocks and even dishes with photos and journaling.

Take Your Pick!

Film canisters, plastic bags, slide mounts, checkbook covers and even dog tags can be manipulated into original works of art! Label and fill a velvet jewelry box with mementos of a 25th wedding anniversary, decorate a small plastic storage case or top a tiny tin to contain a circular album.

A Note About Archival Quality

Sources for Finding and Making Mini Photos

Standard 3½ x 5" or 4 x 6" photo prints will work for a few of the projects in this book, but here are some ideas for creating smaller or even tiny photos:

• Cut out index print photos
• Trim photos from photo booth strips
• Use special instant cameras that print little photos
• Use proofs or the smallest photos from professional portrait packages
• Crop faces and other elements from large or poor photos
• Request small reprints from professional photo labs
• Have contact sheets of your negatives made at a photo lab
• Scan large photos and re-size and reprint them with a personal computer system
• Take shots with a digital camera and print them at reduced sizes
• Scavenge small photos from yearbooks or old I.D. cards

Almost all items produced specifically for scrapbooking are free of acid, lignin and other harmful properties that can discolor or damage your photos and artwork over time. If making your projects of archival quality is a must, be sure to closely read the labels of everything you use. Look for the words *acid-free*, *lignin-free*, *PVC-free*, *permanent*, *fade-resistant* and *waterproof*. Not all materials used on artwork in this book are of archival quality, such as some office supplies, stationery and vintage items. When using these kinds of items, be sure to use copies of your photos as opposed to originals and put a "buffer" of acid-free paper behind any original mementos. Another great way to keep found items from discoloring is to use a commercial de-acidifying spray to neutralize the damaging chemicals in paper products. Mementos such as ticket stubs, pamphlets and receipts may discolor over time, so if this is a concern, include them in clear PVC-free memorabilia pockets, or use color copies, making sure to make the copies on acid-free paper. A primary tip for extending the life of your work is to exclusively use quality adhesives made specifically for memory crafts because of their archival qualities. Since the projects in this book are meant to be handled and enjoyed, be sure to use enough adhesive to securely adhere all the elements. When your finished projects are not on display, keep them in a "safe" container that will protect them from light and moisture and find a spot to store them that will be free of extreme environmental changes.

More Theme Ideas For Mini Memory Projects

- **ADMIRE ARCHITECTURE** *Include shots of interesting buildings and structures from a trip or from your own town or city.*

- **CAPTURE COLOR** *Create an album containing photos of items in your life that are all the same color.*

- **CHERISH CHUMS** *Gather photos of all your friends throughout childhood.*

- **CLIP CARDS** *Gather up old I.D. cards and bind them into a book of potentially embarrassing photos.*

- **COLLECT CARDS** *Bind together the holiday cards you receive or send each year, along with the senders' or your own family's holiday portrait.*

- **COMPARE CHANGES** *Make an album based on before-and-after photos of a home project, a makeover, the cleanup of a muddy kid or pet, etc.*

- **CONTAIN CORSAGES** *Make a keepsake container to preserve and protect small flower corsages from special occasions.*

- **CREATE CAPSULES** *Make mini time capsules to be sealed and opened in the future.*

- **CORRAL CORRESPONDENCE** *Decorate a small box to hold your child's holiday wish lists and letters to Santa.*

- **DESIGN DECORATIONS** *Use favorite photos to create unique ornaments for your Christmas tree.*

- **DISPLAY DIGITS** *Make a book filled with photos of all your family members' hands.*

- **DOCUMENT DINNERS** *To create a fun food time capsule, record a week's worth of your family's meals with photos and journaling, both at home and at restaurants.*

- **ENCASE EGGS** *Photograph Easter eggs each family member decorated.*

- **EXHIBIT EVENTS** *Along with photos, fill a little album with the receipts, tickets, program and other mementos of an event you attended, such as a concert or play.*

- **FEATURE FLASHBACKS** *List toys you had, TV shows you watched and clothes you wore as a kid.*

- **FILE FASHIONS** *Collect photos of your outdated outfits and hairdos over the years.*

- **FOOL FRIENDS** *Replace the contents of Valentine's candy boxes with custom albums.*

- **GATHER GIFTS** *List gifts you have received or those you have made for others.*

- **LIST LIKES** *Make pages with corresponding photos listing favorite hobbies, music, food, movies and more.*

- **MAINTAIN MESSAGES** *Fill a small book with notes from friends you saved from childhood, or everyday notes your family has written to you.*

- **PORTRAY PAJAMAS** *Craft a cute collection of family members in their favorite pj's.*

- **PRESENT PICTURES** *Burn a CD or DVD of photos and place them in a case with a custom cover and title for a gift.*

- **PRESERVE PLACES** *Capture photos of favorite places in your neighborhood.*

- **PRIZE PICTURES** *Assemble a project featuring your annual family portrait.*

- **REMEMBER ROOMS** *Save hotel key cards and bind them into a little album with photos from each trip.*

- **REVISIT RESIDENCES** *Include past addresses and when you lived there with photos of the buildings.*

- **SALUTE SEASONS** *Capture changing images of your garden or home during different times of the year.*

- **SAVE SALUTATIONS** *Organize all your letters and e-mails from a much-loved friend or relative.*

- **SHOWCASE STUFF** *Make mini museums documenting the contents of your closet, refrigerator or purse.*

- **STORE SOUVENIRS** *Decorate and label small containers filled with sand from a beach vacation, confetti from a special event or other small mementos.*

- **SURPRISE SOMEONE** *Create an album and hide it to be discovered later in his or her lunch bag, briefcase or home.*

- **TRACK TREES** *Take a photo of your Christmas tree each year and add it to a small scrapbook.*

- **TREAT TRICKSTERS** *For a party favor, take an instant photo of each costumed attendee at a Halloween party (or of the whole group) and attach it to a decorated card.*

- **VIEW VALENTINES** *Make albums containing your or your child's Valentine cards each year.*

- **WELCOME WISHES** *Save cards made by your children and include dates and ages.*

Chapter one

Family and Friends

CELEBRATE COMPANIONS

Adorn friendship albums with glittered letters

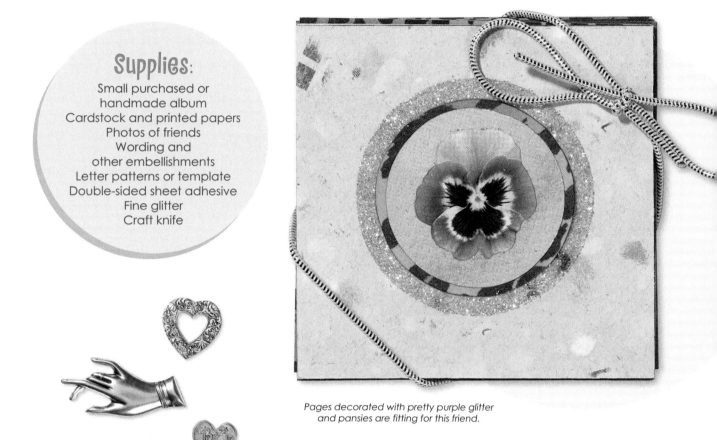

Supplies:
Small purchased or
handmade album
Cardstock and printed papers
Photos of friends
Wording and
other embellishments
Letter patterns or template
Double-sided sheet adhesive
Fine glitter
Craft knife

*Pages decorated with pretty purple glitter
and pansies are fitting for this friend.*

A great way to pay tribute to a special person in your life is to handcraft a small album commemorating your friendship. Make one for yourself as a keepsake, for an unforgettable gift for your friend, or make a matched pair so you both can have one to enjoy! Accordion-style albums work well because you can add names and words that can be read when the album is opened. Plus, they are easy to stand up on a shelf or desk for display. Spell out "friends" or your pal's name on each page using the pretty glittered technique shown here. Include current photos of your friend and list his or her traits, or use photos from over the years, adding the dates they were taken. You can also theme your album around favorite photos of you and your friend together. Incorporate one photo from each year you've known each other for a fun timeline of your friendship, or show pictures of the two of you doing what you enjoy together, like sports, crafts, eating, shopping, etc. Add appropriate words describing your friendship to finish an album you and your friend will always treasure.

More Ideas:

Try sprinkling several different colors of glitter on each letter for a varied effect.

Instead of using sheet adhesive to make the letters, use a fine-point glue pen to trace printed letters or letter stickers, then apply the glitter while the glue is still wet.

If spelling your friend's name, add traits that start with the same letter on each page of the album, such as S for smart, U for understanding, Z for zany, etc.

To add a more masculine treatment to the letters, use metallic or dark-colored micro beads instead of sparkly glitter.

Experiment with gold or silver leafing in place of glitter.

Besides lettering, try this technique with designs as well. Handcut them or use paper punches.

Include journaling describing your friend or the situations behind the photos. A good place for this is on the back of the accordion album pages.

For a fun friendship theme, add photos and wording about "inside" jokes or memories that you share.

Apply glittered letters on greeting cards for a pretty touch.

Use this technique for projects about other subjects. Simply spell out appropriate words like MOM or PARTY.

Fill a blank book with photos and journaling about all of your current friends, or about all of your past friends, beginning with childhood.

Add extra flair to your letters by trimming away the covering paper of the sheet adhesive in stages, adding glitter of a different color each time.

Here's how to create the glittered letters:

1 Copy or print patterns for each letter being used. Staple them one at a time to trimmed pieces of double-sided sheet adhesive, then use a craft knife to carefully cut out each letter. Note: Alphabet templates can be used to trace letter patterns directly onto the sheet adhesive.

2 Peel the backing paper from the sheet adhesive and adhere the letters directly to your project.

3 Use the tip of a craft knife to carefully peel the thick covering paper on the letters, then apply a liberal coating of glitter over the exposed adhesive. Shake off the excess glitter and if necessary, use a small soft paintbrush to brush away any that clings to the paper around the letters. Use a craft tray to catch the excess glitter to make cleanup easy.

PRAISE PARENTS

Bind mother and father books with border stickers

Photos of your mother changing over the years also capture changing fashions and trends.

Who is more deserving of his or her own special album than a parent? Whether these albums feature your parents or celebrate the father or mother of your own children, they are a wonderful way to express just how important parents are to their families. Create a book depicting your mom or dad over the years, make a father/daughter or mother/son album with favorite pictures of the two together, or fill an album with photos of a new dad and his baby to commemorate his first year as a father. For yet another option, make albums for your grown children who are now parents themselves. After choosing your subjects and reproducing select photos, gather tags or other small items to bind into an album. Determine your color scheme and locate complementary border or block stickers, then bind and decorate the small pages. Once completed, these little books make great Mother's Day or Father's Day gifts, but it's just as nice to make them for yourself as a reminder of how much you love your parents and how much they love you.

Supplies:

Tags or other small items for pages
Border or block stickers
Photos of parents
Printed papers and other embellishments
Ruler
Pencil

Slide mounts and other small items can easily be bound using this technique.

More ideas:

Besides binding with border and block stickers, try using one large object sticker or several small ones, such as flowers, to do the job.

Try decorative or foil tapes in place of stickers for binding.

Use ephemera, playing cards, laminate chips, thin wood shapes or even metal mesh for pages.

Use several short horizontal border sticker strips for the binding instead of long, vertical ones.

Instead of stickers, try this same binding technique with cut paper. Just be sure to use sheet adhesive or another adhesive that covers the entire back surface of the paper pieces.

If you're a parent, make little albums featuring you with each child and keep them as mementos, or give them to your children as gifts.

Use faux metallic border stickers to bind a book about your best buddy.

Here's how to bind the books:

1 Measure the sticker to determine half its width and use that measurement to mark a line on one side of each tag. Note: It's best to decorate the backgrounds of each page before this step.

2 Apply a small block sticker or section of a border sticker in alignment with the line. Cut long border stickers into shorter lengths before binding the album and trim away any excess that may extend beyond the top and bottom edges of the pages.

3 Adhere a second tag to the remainder of the exposed sticker, leaving a 1/16" gap between the ends of the tags.

4 Fold the two tags together so the front of the sticker is on the inside. Then, line up and adhere another sticker and tag. Repeat the above steps until the book has the number of desired pages. To finish the binding, wrap a sticker around the spine of the book and decorate the album pages.

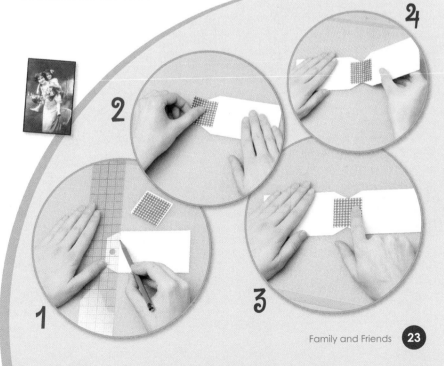

HERALD HERITAGE

Create timeless jewelry with vintage photos and modern findings

Glaze paper and tiny photos to small metal tags for a pair of fun earrings.

Add micro beads to the glaze while still wet to add texture to the collage.

Craft a pretty choker that features your mother when she was young.

Honor beloved relatives by creating handmade jewelry portraits that you can wear close to your heart. Choose from the multitude of blank jewelry, mini frames and charms available, from costume metals to real silver or gold. Combine them with heritage photos and attractive papers to craft unique earrings, pins, bracelets and necklaces. A quick coating of commercial paper glaze is all it takes to form a protective seal over the small collages. To adorn these wearable works of art, select jewels or charms that fit the personality of the individual featured, and tie a little frame onto a string of pretty beads to form a necklace. For earrings, attach hooks, and for brooches, use glue-on pin backs. Once completed, you'll find your customized jewelry is beautiful and durable enough to be worn and enjoyed every day and makes for wonderful gifts and engaging conversation starters.

Supplies:
Metal frames and charms
Decorative paper scraps
Reduced copies of vintage photos
Jewelry findings: earring hooks,
pin backs, beading cord,
crimp beads, jump rings
Beads and rhinestones
Paper glaze
Paintbrush
Needle-nose pliers
Double-sided sheet
adhesive
Wet adhesive

More ideas:

Use tiny letters to add names or words to these mini portraits.

Try this project using contemporary color portraits as well as still life and landscape scenes.

Customize vintage jewelry pieces in addition to new frames and charms.

String necklaces with metal chain in place of beads.

Add dimension to the glaze finish by applying several thicker coats.

Create texture and patterns in the glaze finish with exaggerated brushstrokes.

Utilize these little pieces as embellishments for scrapbooks and other paper crafts.

Fashion a funky pin by turning a frame charm upside down and dangling a cool shoe charm from it.

Instead of paper glaze, clear epoxy stickers can be used as a protective coating on the jewelry.

Here's how to make the necklace:

1 Trim printed paper to fit the jewelry piece and adhere it with sheet adhesive.

2 Silhouette cut a reduced copy of a family photo and smoothly adhere it to the papered jewelry piece.

3 Use a small, flat paintbrush to apply paper glaze over the little collage. You may add tiny glass beads or glitter to the glaze while still wet for further adornment. Allow the piece to dry overnight and add small rhinestones if desired.

4 Loop stretchy illusion cord through the charm and string the beads up both sides. Finish the ends of the beaded cord by threading both through a bead that has been crimped shut with jewelry pliers. Trim away the excess cord. Note: The stretchy cord allows the choker length necklace to fit over the head without a clasp.

PROTECT PETS

Bind pet albums with colorful paper clips

Say the word "clip" around your pets and they'll probably take off running, but the colorful paper and binder clips used in this project are nothing to be afraid of! Paper clips and binder clips come in a myriad of colors, shapes and sizes, from standard silver to every color of the rainbow, as well as round shapes, heart shapes and even clips with decorative charms attached. Choose clips and papers that work best for your pal's personality and that's all you need to create a custom, easy-to-adorn album. Begin by determining the size you would like the album to be and trim all papers accordingly. You may also use ready-cut stationery or notecards for the pages. If the papers are white on the reverse side, they can be smoothly adhered together with sheet adhesive prior to binding, which helps to stiffen thin paper. (If double-sided cardstock is being used, this step isn't necessary). It's easiest to decorate the album while the pages are unassembled, so do this before attaching the clips. Clip-style binding is especially handy because it allows you to quickly add or change pages whenever you'd like.

Supplies:
Printed papers or stationery
Photos of pets
Flat or binder paper clips
Clear grid ruler
Scoring tool
Dry adhesive
Wording
Accents

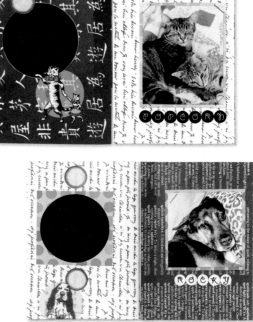

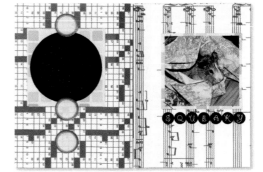

Add journaling to describe how your pet came into, or out of, your life.

More ideas:

Try different sizes or shapes for each page to achieve a fun, free-form look.

Try binding ephemera, vellum, transparencies or even cloth for cool pages.

Make separate albums for each pet, or combine them in one chronological book.

Create a tribute album after the passing of a pet to aid in coping with the loss.

Make a book about a friend's beloved pet for an unexpected gift.

Use this technique to craft unique greeting cards with paper clip binding.

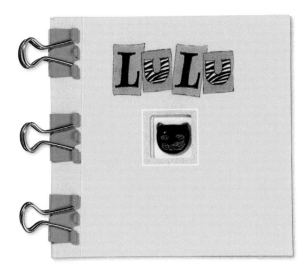

Bind mini note cards with mini binder clips for a perfect little album.

Colorful note cards make quick pages for a cute book about a cat.

tigger

The house cats sits and smiles and sings. She knows a lot of secret things.
-Annette Wynne

Here's how to bind the albums:

1 Stack the pages in the desired order and temporarily attach one clip to the left-hand side to measure the "reach" of the clips. Remove the clip and use a clear ruler and scoring tool to lightly score each page.

2 Use your fingers or a bone folder to slightly fold the spine forward on of all the pages.

3 Re-stack the pages and simply place the clips along the spine to bind the album.

LOG LIFE

Create custom titles and embellishments with magazine clippings

This teen's journal makes use of her quickly outdated fashion magazines.

Supplies:

Old magazines or catalogs
Double-sided adhesive
Purchased or handmade album
Photos representative of the subject's life
Printed papers
Embellishments
Alphabet or design template
Scissors and craft knife
Fine-tipped permanent marker

This project is a great way to utilize old magazines and catalogs for adorning journals celebrating your life or the life of someone else. Make an album highlighting the important aspects of your own life or, for a fun gift, have the recipient add his or her own journaling and photos. To start, buy or make a small album. A book of CD pocket sleeves bound with binder rings is a perfect present or craft project for "'tweens" and teens. Punch holes for binding the sleeves together, and leave the pockets unsealed for slipping photos, journaling or mementos inside to show through the windows. Add headings and decorations to each page, then create a custom title to adorn the cover.

For another idea for a handmade album that utilizes your old magazines and catalogs, use a metal-edged ruler and craft knife and measure and cut a small "book" from the spine edge of the magazine. It will take several passes of the craft knife to cut through all the pages, and if the magazine being used is bound only with staples, make sure at least one of them is centered on the spine of your little album to keep it intact. Label and decorate the pages and utilize the same patchwork technique as above, but instead cut a flower or other image to adorn the cover. Besides decorating little life journals, these collaged letters and designs can be customized for any of your scrapbooking or paper crafting projects.

Cut out a small album along the spine of a catalog or magazine and decorate the cover with a cute flower made from clippings.

More ideas:

Another good title for an album like this is "All About Me!"

Make one comprehensive album that covers all aspects of your life, including friends, family, home and hobbies. Or, make a separate little book for each and store them together in a labeled container.

Include only current information about your life, making sure to add the date the book was created. Or create an album celebrating your entire life, including lists for all the schools you attended, all your past boyfriends, jobs, etc.

If presenting a blank "Log of Life" as a gift, include a nice pen and perhaps some adhesive so the album is ready for the recipient to use.

Try using printed papers or elements of your own photos in place of magazine clippings for lettering and embellishments.

Experiment with paper punches and freehand cutting in addition to utilizing templates.

Any simple shape can make a great accent. See pg. 94 for patterns.

Here's how to create the letters and embellishments:

1 Cut small elements of colorful prints and patterns from magazine pages. Next, cut a piece of double-sided sheet adhesive that is slightly larger than the letter you are making and peel off one side of the backing. Lay the clippings one at a time onto the exposed adhesive, creating a patchwork that covers the entire piece. You may need to trim some clippings as you go to better fit the exposed sections of adhesive.

2 Use an alphabet template or other pattern to trace a reverse image of the letter or design onto the remaining backing of the sheet adhesive.

3 Cut out the letter or design, then use the tip of a craft knife to carefully peel off the backing. Then, adhere it wherever you would like it to be on your project.

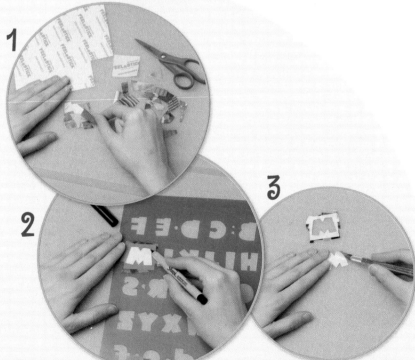

MAGNETIZE MEMORIES

Turn favorite photos into fun refrigerator magnets

A heart shape works great for a photo of a couple in love.

Who doesn't have at least a few magnets or mementos on the front of their fridge door? Take down tired old magnets, spare your favorite photos unnecessary food stains and create an impromptu kitchen gallery with this easy project. A few inexpensive supplies and copies of photos are all you need to make durable and unique magnets for yourself or for gifts. Start by gathering photos of family, friends or pets. Make copies, reducing a photo's size when necessary. Find printed papers and accents that will help convey the style you desire, whether retro, vintage, French country or the like. If you're making this project for a friend, keep his or her home/kitchen décor in mind while determining your design. Create a fun collage on wooden shapes and follow the simple steps shown to add a protective coating to complete the magnets. Make a bunch and get ready to make over your refrigerator door!

Supplies:
Wooden craft shapes
Photos of family and friends
Printed paper and/or stickers
Printed words or alphabet stickers
Clear embossing ink
Clear embossing powder
3D accents
Magnets
Sheet adhesive
Glue
Craft knife
Heat tool

For a magnet of a cute child in your life, decorate it with stickers that match his or her personality.

Don't forget to make magnets featuring your favorite pets!

For a gift for a family member, make a magnet using a photo from his or her childhood.

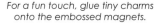

For a fun touch, glue tiny charms onto the embossed magnets.

More ideas:

Use black or white foam core instead of the wooden shapes.

Use sheet laminate as a durable alternative to wet embossing.

Feature photos from vacations for magnets that double as souvenirs.

Cut cute phrases from books or magazines for your magnet's wording.

Instead of photos, use letter stickers or alphabet stamps to create fun word magnets.

Experiment with the embossing powder coating by using extra thick embossing powders or by adding glitter while heat-setting.

Save freebie magnets from realtors or pizza delivery places to cut and use for the magnetic backing.

Make some magnets for your kids' lockers or an office filing cabinet.

Customize the theme of the magnets for memorable party favors.

Use this technique for making great jewelry pins as well.

A pretty magnet made with a heritage photo would look nice in a studio or office as well as on the fridge.

Smaller magnets are great for holding up notes on metal bulletin boards.

Photograph flowers or other objects to adorn your magnets.

In place of photos, use real or reproduction ephemera on your magnets and wrap them in clear cellophane for a great hospitality or housewarming gift.

Here's how to make the magnets:

1 Color the edges of the wooden shapes with paint or markers if desired. Apply sheet adhesive to one side of the shape, trim the excess and remove the backing.

2 Smoothly adhere printed papers to the exposed adhesive and trim the excess. Apply stickers if desired, then cut out the photo and adhere it to the paper. Apply letter stickers or printed words as well.

3 Cover the entire front surface with clear embossing ink by pressing an inkpad over the entire piece. Use firm pressure to assure complete coverage of the wet ink.

4 Immediately cover the wet ink with clear embossing powder, shaking off any excess. Set ink with a heat tool specifically designed for crafting. Note: Some paper items can buckle under the heat. To avoid this, keep the heat tool moving and don't hold it too close to your artwork.

5 For a finishing touch, glue a few fun accents on top. Firmly glue a magnet to the back and allow it to dry 24 hours before use.

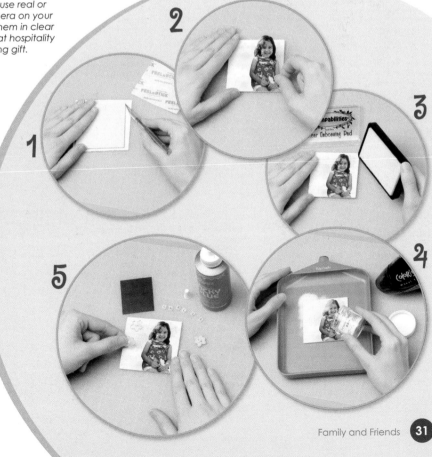

REMEMBER REUNIONS

Bind blank cards with bands for reunion keepsakes

Cherries and crackle paint are proper adornments for memories of a country reunion.

It used to be that a rubber band was just that: a rubber band. Nowadays you can take your pick from numerous materials and styles. Stretchy plastic bands are available in a wide variety of colors, some of which even feature striped patterns. Binding little books and albums with bands is so easy you could use the technique for a project of any theme. It works especially well for events where you will have accumulated photos and lots of miscellaneous mementos and notes, such as family and school reunions.

Start by buying or making blank greeting cards. Leave them plain or layer their covers and pages with printed papers and stamped designs. You may add images and other embellishments at this point if you'd like, but it's easy to add more once the album is assembled. For a family reunion album, include pages for the invitation and map, new addresses you gathered, recipes for potluck dishes served and, of course, for photos. For a high school reunion, add your tickets and journaling about the events that took place. This project can be easily adapted for creating reunion invitations as well. Just include the time and location on one page and tuck in a map, a blank name tag and an RSVP card. Label the remaining pages for recipes, addresses and photos, and every guest will have a keepsake album ready to fill with memories of the reunion.

Supplies:

Blank cards
Plastic "rubber" bands
or hair bands
Photos from reunions
Mementos
Printed papers
Wording
Embellishments

For a quick high school reunion album, stack several cards inside one another and bind the spines with colorful plastic bands.

More ideas:

For especially fast and easy binding, "nest" all of the cards inside one another and use one or more bands to attach them together at their spines.

Make reduced copies of original photos and memorabilia if you wish to keep originals separate or in case they don't fit inside a mini album.

Leave room to write directly onto pages while at the picnic or party.

Trim each card to a different height or length before binding.

Use decorative scissors to cut patterns on the edges of each page.

Bind albums by tying decorative fibers around the spines in place of bands.

For particularly funky binding, use a frilly or flowery hair band or "scrunchie" in place of bands.

Use bands to archive greeting cards.

Note: Real rubber bands usually harden and crack over time, so avoid using them for this project.

Here's how to build a book with bands:

1 Stack two cards and stretch a band around the back half of one card and the front half of the second, carefully securing the band around the spines of the cards.

2 Stretch another band between the two cards and around the spine. To add more pages, simply repeat these steps in accordance with the number of pages.

3 Wrap an additional band around each page to create a holder to tuck loose photos and mementos into, allowing original items to be included without permanently adhering them to the pages.

4 Secure the album closed by wrapping bands around the outside.

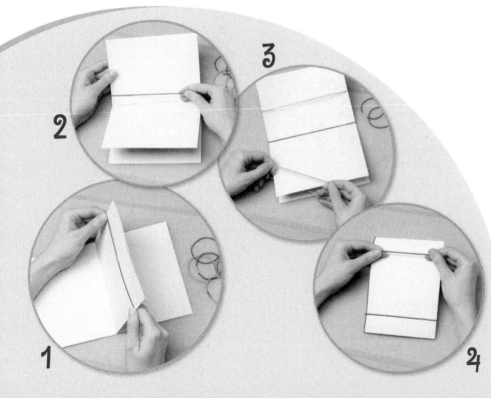

DOCUMENT DAYS

Make "ordinary" days special with little albums

Use stencils to spell out the special day you are featuring.

Make a colorful little album from envelopes to feature the details of your typical day.

It's almost automatic to take photos during holidays and other big events, but don't forget to capture just how special everyday occurrences are too. The precious details of your daily life can change so fast, but with a few dated records, they won't be forgotten with time. There are many "uneventful" themes that these little books can be based on. Use alphabet stencils to make the pages of a fold-out album spell a day of the week. List your family's typical way to spend that day, adding photos accordingly. Or, pick a weekday and spell out everything that happened to you or the whole family each hour of the day, from getting up until going to bed. Designate a day that your family spends apart, and in separate notebooks, have all members describe their own day. Include a photo of each person and also add any other pictures taken. Read the journals together right away, then store them to be enjoyed years into the future.

Sometimes something so simple as the weather can make a day memorable. Take photos to document a beautiful day, a blizzard or a big thunderstorm. You can also add pictures of the way your family enjoyed it or survived it. You might also feature a routine trip to the park or zoo in individual mini albums. Once you get started, it may be hard to stop thinking of "typical" days you want to pay tribute to. No matter how many you make, be sure to bring these little time capsules out once in awhile to wonder at the ways you and your family have changed and the ways you have stayed the same.

Supplies:

Small purchased or handmade album
Photos of family on designated days
Wording
Embellishments

More ideas:

Instant photos are an easy way to take pictures throughout the day and quickly add them to your project.

To enhance your album, include the day's weather statistics and even copies of newspaper clippings.

Once each year, list the details of your child's normal day with photos and mementos, and present the gift album to him or her upon high school graduation.

Document a normal, non-holiday visit with the grandparents, and make two albums—one for the grandchild and one for the grandparents.

Take your camera to work, capture your day away from home and turn it into a book that can be shared now or in the future.

Make an album that includes photos from one day for each season of that year showing your house and yard and how your family is dressed to go out.

Record a day in the life of your pet, even if half the photos are of him or her just sleeping around the house.

Use applicable items for your albums' pages, such as faux money for a book about a yard sale or flash cards for an album about a day at school.

A folded "cootie catcher" is a great foundation for photos of a day trip with kids.

This tiny album and mini magnifying glass are the ticket to revisiting the images of a beautiful fall day.

Time and sentiment turn heritage photos of an "uneventful" jaunt into a terrific tag album.

Make a small gift album for a friend celebrating the day or night you traditionally spend together.

Create a fun time capsule where each person writes down how he or she spent the same day.

Chapter two

Events and Celebrations

FRAME FLOWERS

Sandwich flower photos between pretty paper frames

Capture the beauty of your garden so it can be savored again and again.

Like snowflakes, no two flowers are exactly alike. Similarly, the "life span" of each is extremely short. This project provides a way to save and remember special flowers, whether they are from your garden or from beautiful gift bouquets. Photograph prized flowers and plants in your garden and make an album for each year, or just make one that you can add a page or two to each season. To add detail to these pages, consider including smaller dried flowers, individual petals and leaves from the same plant. If you're lucky enough to have flowers delivered to you on occasions such as anniversaries, birthdays, new jobs or new babies, be sure to take photos of them for an album full of beautiful, everlasting bouquets. Add journaling indicating the occasion, the date and who sent them. If you enjoy taking photographs of favorite flowers on walks or vacations, turn them into a fun little book as well. A quick and fitting way to organize all these pretty pictures is to place them between purchased or handcut paper frames. Refer to the simple steps shown for details, then start creating an archive of beautiful flowers before they are gone forever.

More ideas:

Include the little cards that accompanied your gift bouquets.

Use a small real frame to adorn the cover of a flower album.

Create your own frames from cardstock, tags, seed packets or thin wood veneer.

Utilize slide mounts for the frames on each page and bind them together.

Take photos of full-sized picture frames and reduce them.

Document all the wonderful flowers at a wedding by including photos of the arrangements, the bride's bouquet, the groom's corsage and those worn by the wedding party.

Make an album showcasing the bountiful results of a vegetable garden.

Apply this technique to make unique greeting cards, scrapbook page embellishments and "sun catchers."

Simply frame small photos for a mini book feauring your favorite flower.

Show your honey how much you appreciate his thoughtfulness by making a permanent vignette featuring his present.

Here's how to make the framed pages:

1 Trim two pieces of a transparency so that they are slightly smaller than the paper frame. Use mounting squares to attach one to the back of the frame.

2 Crop two photos so that they are exactly the same size and adhere them back to back. Then, use a mounting square to tack one corner of the double-sided photo to the frame. Apply a tiny dot of glue to each dried element using a toothpick and place them onto the transparent window.

3 Peel the backing from the mounting squares and adhere the second piece of transparency over the photos and dried elements. To finish the page, use additional mounting squares to adhere a second identical frame faceup over the first. To bind the album, punch a hole in the upper left corner of each page and attach them together with rings, chain or fibers.

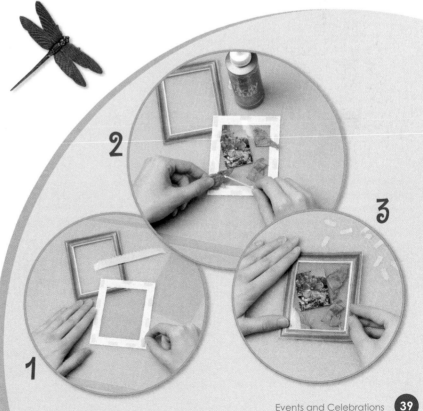

REQUEST RSVPS

Fashion one-of-a-kind party invitations with papers and swizzle sticks

Design the invitations with the same motif as the party.

Make the invitations as memorable as the party itself with this fun project! Swizzle sticks, both vintage and new, are available in many designs and may be purchased at party supply stores, gift shops, paper catalogs, online catalogs and even antique stores and flea markets. After selecting sticks and papers that best suit your party's theme, follow steps 1 through 3. It's easiest to adhere the wording and any other elements prior to binding the pages together. Try alphabet stickers and stamps or use your computer to print the party's time, location and other information. Include a photo of the guest of honor, or leave room for a picture to be taken during the event. Add stickers and other quick embellishments if desired and finish the invitations by following step 4. These can be made fairly quickly and inexpensively in numbers, but you may want to hand deliver them to assure safe arrival. Protect your creations during mailing by purchasing colorful padded envelopes (extra postage may be required). In addition to invitations, try using this technique to create little party albums perfect for adding photos and journaling to for remembering the festivities long after the guests have gone home.

Supplies:
Craft or scrapbooking papers
Swizzle sticks or party picks
Photos (optional)
Wording
Stickers and other accents (optional)
Circle cutter
Hole punch
Dry adhesive

More ideas:

Try other shapes in addition to circles for the pages.

Punch small squares, hearts or stars for the holes.

For fun favors, take an instant photo of each party guest that can be added to a blank page in his or her invitation.

Try this binding technique using pencils, paintbrushes, sticks, chopsticks, bamboo skewers and long matches.

To complete the party theme, use the same swizzle sticks or picks in drinks or as decorations at the event.

Party picks are fun to use too. Add a mini photo from the party to create a small token of the night.

Using swizzle sticks doesn't limit this project to adult events—this pink flamingo is fitting for a little girl's slumber party.

Here's how to make the invitations:

1 Cut two 5" circles and one 5 ³/₈" circle from printed papers, or make them approximately 1" shorter than the swizzle stick being used.

2 Adhere the two 5" circles back to back to reveal only the patterned side of the papers. The invitations can have just two pages as shown here, or add several more. It adds a little something extra if the back page is slightly larger than the rest to create a border.

3 Stack the pages in order and use a paper punch to punch an even number of holes down one side. It is helpful to cut a pattern from scratch paper to measure the placement of the holes first, but "eyeballing" them works fine as they needn't be exact.

4 Once the pages are decorated, re-stack them and carefully weave the swizzle stick through the holes.

INSTILL INSPIRATION

Create photo backgrounds for little quote books

the sky is the limit!

chase life

live your passion

ATTITUDE is everything

Express Yourself

imagine

create

dream

inspire

hope

Supplies:
Photos of flowers, leaves, stones, etc.
Computer, printer and photo software (optional)
Small album or box
Printed quotes or sayings
Printed papers and other embellishments

Encourage a graduate with a box of uplifting advice.

There are many mini gift books on the market, but sometimes it's hard to find one that is ideal for your particular occasion. Creating a personalized book of inspiring quotes or advice is an especially meaningful gesture any recipient will appreciate. Give graduates a positive outlook on their future with a small box filled with blue skies and encouraging statements, or make a little book for newly-weds full of handwritten marital advice from their friends and families. A book that lists reasons why life is good makes a thoughtful gift for a friend's birthday or someone's retirement. You can even use a little album to send your thoughts of sympathy and support to a widow or to cheer up someone who is ill or recently divorced.

To truly make these books unique, start by taking specific photographs to decorate their covers and pages. Subjects from nature such as leaves, flowers and clouds are great options, but also look for interesting textures, patterns, or even use photos of houses and people. In addition, experiment with altering your photographs by printing them at less than 100% opacity for softness, or use filters on your camera or computer to slightly distort them. After printing and trimming the pages to size, buy or make a little book or tuck the pages into small containers. Adhere the cropped photos to each page and add quotes, sayings, advice and adornments to finish a gift that will encourage and inspire for years to come.

More ideas:

Look through photos you already have for portions you can scan, reprint and use.

Announce your pregnancy to your parents by presenting them with a little book of quotes about grandparents and see how long it takes for the news to register.

Decorate a valentine "conversation hearts" candy box with the title "52 Reasons I Love You" and fill it with 52 pages or cards listing why.

Capture someone's personality by filling pages with his or her own favorite or funny sayings.

Create a book of quotes about cats or dogs for a proud new pet owner.

Try taking photos purposely out of focus for more abstract backgrounds.

Use your computer to add text to photos before you print them.

Use tiny envelopes as your pages and tuck a little card with a quote into each one. Seal each envelope and add dates for when they each are to be opened.

Make use of fun candy containers and small tins to house pages.

Make up your own quotes, or use those of friends and family if you can't find existing ones that fit.

Color photos, black-and-white photos and altered photos all work for this project.

A cute box of jokes will cheer up a buddy who's blue.

Cover a circle album of motivational sayings with a colorful flower for a gift that will surely lift spirits.

Hand-color a landscape photo to decorate a list of things to be grateful for, such as friends, family, home, good food, etc. Use corresponding photos for the background of each entry.

Soft photos of plants comprise a pretty background for a little book of encouraging quotes.

VISIT VACATIONS

Use coasters as covers for travel albums

This little album reminisces a romantic island vacation.

Relive a wonderful vacation any time and place by creating a small album that can easily be carried with you or displayed on your desk at home or work. Sure, you could purchase a plain album to fill with your memories, but why not make a custom one as memorable as your trip? Drink coasters make unique and durable covers for just such an album. Available in many colors and designs, it is easy to find coasters that will fit the theme of any trip. Cardboard, cork, foam, wood and even plastic coasters will work for this project. Find them in gift, kitchen, discount and department stores. Even better, purchase them during the actual vacation at souvenir shops or save the free drink mats from cafes, bars or restaurants visited. A few simple steps are all it takes to turn these tokens of travel into little albums featuring photos and mementos from your trip.

An easy way to use a coaster for a cover is to simply adhere it to the front of a small purchased album.

More ideas:

Cut a "window" in the front coaster to frame a dimensional memento.

Adhere accordion pages between two coasters instead of binding pages through holes.

Use ceramic or glass coasters by simply attaching a purchased or handmade album between them in place of drilling.

Of course, you can try this coaster cover technique for albums of any subject!

Try this same binding technique using metal or wood crafting shapes as album covers.

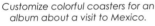

Customize colorful coasters for an album about a visit to Mexico.

Black foam coasters are fitting for a book about a fun road trip.

Bind vintage milk caps for an extra-tiny album.

Here's how to bind the albums:

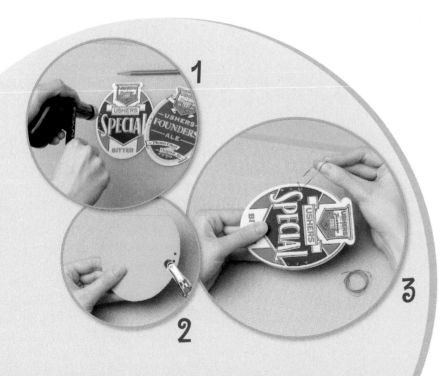

1 Choose two identically shaped coasters and measure and mark the locations of the desired number of holes about ¼" in along one side of each. Use a hand drill to drill the holes into both coasters. (If using a rounded coaster, only drill one to three holes very close together so you will be able to open the album after binding).

2 To create the pages, trace the shape of the coaster onto cardstock and cut the desired number of pages. If desired, you can also make the pages slightly undersized. Next, use one of the drilled coasters as a pattern to mark the location of the holes on each page. Use a hole punch to punch all of them.

3 Align the pages between the two coasters and use wire, jump rings, binder rings, bead chain or fibers to bind them together through each hole. To allow the pages to open completely, make sure not to bind them too tightly. Finish the album by decorating the cover and pages with photos, journaling and embellishments.

RECORD ROMANCE

Fill shadow boxes with special photos and mementos

Celebrate soul mates with a colorful collage.

Supplies:

Shadow box or other
small container
Printed papers
Photo of couple
Memorabilia
Dimensional adhesive shapes
Charms and other
embellishments
Dimensional adhesive
and glue
Ruler

This project is a fun way to recall romantic occasions you'll never want to forget, such as weddings, anniversaries or a special night spent together. Small shadow boxes are perfect for display in your home or office and make unique, memorable gifts. Combine a wedding photo with elements of the invitation and wedding decor to create a one-of-a-kind memento or gift. Build a box with anniversary photos to document your own milestone or those of loved ones. Find funny photos from a date with your husband and surprise him with a blast from the past, or enclose mementos from an unforgettable evening, such as a matchbook from the restaurant you dined at or ticket stubs from an event you attended. For another meaningful idea, use heritage photos to honor a great couple from your family.

Start by purchasing a shadow box frame or other small container that opens and has a clear lid. Line the inside back of the box with printed paper, a fun collage, or paper of your own design created with stamps and ink. Use dimensional adhesive to adhere photos, mementos and charms at varying depths by layering from the background out. Complete the shadow box by adding names, dates, places and embellishments to the outside of the box if desired. Hang the shadow box on a wall, rest it on a desk, or add it to a display on a mantel or dresser. These petite shadow boxes can be perched most anywhere and serve as daily reminders of true love.

More ideas:

Decorate the frames of purchased shadow boxes with additional words or charms.

Line the back of clear containers with printed transparencies.

Use a solvent-based inkpad to stamp permanent images on the clear box lids.

For an unforgettable anniversary gift, make an individual shadow box representing each decade a couple has been married.

Use a clear storage box with several compartments and fill each "room" with a picture and memento from a different year or event.

Create mini shadow boxes for other occasions such as vacations, pets or friendships.

Present mini shadow boxes as Valentine's Day gifts for your mate.

Make shadow box magnets and jewelry from tiny containers and tins.

Experiment with these ideas using full-size shadow box frames.

Construct a tiny world of flowers and butterflies for a whimsical grandparent shadow box.

A round storage tin makes a nice shadow "box" too.

Add mini copies of photo booth pictures to a thin plastic case for a simple and sweet shadow box.

Use a wedding invitation and matching décor to make a memento of the big day.

Decorate a tiny colored container to hold souvenir coins and other mementos from romantic trips and dates.

LAVISH LUCK

Bestow good-luck wishes with fun fortune books

Supplies:
Small album
Photos of people or items associated with luck
Printed papers
Fortunes or printed words
Plastic craft lens or bottle cap
Charm or other small dimensional item
Glitter or micro beads
Clear-drying glue
Rhinestones and other accents (optional)

Vintage pictures matted with glitter give style to your good wishes.

LIVE WELL

Fame, riches and romance are yours for the asking.
Lucky Numbers 10, 20, 25, 30, 40, 45

Even if you don't like the taste of fortune cookies, it's always fun to read the little slip of paper inside, and who wouldn't save a four-leaf clover if they happened to find one? Use these little icons of luck to decorate small albums and cards filled with good fortune. Give them to wish a friend "bon voyage" for an adventurous trip or to tell a departing co-worker goodbye and good luck. You can use purchased fortune stickers or print your own to express best wishes for newlyweds or others in the midst of life-changing events. You can also simply save your own Chinese food fortunes for fun, or for use in later projects.

To decorate the cover of a fortune-filled book, start by looking for a charm that represents good luck; choose from four-leaf clovers, horseshoes, wishbones, a shiny penny, the number 7, etc. Next, purchase a domed plastic lens sold for paper crafting, or simply recycle a bottle cap or small lid. Follow the steps shown to combine the charm and lens into a unique embellishment. Once assembled, adhere it to the album cover and add wings or other accents around it for an additional touch. Decorate the pages of the project with pictures and well-wishes or fortunes and it will be ready to grant good luck to a deserving recipient.

More ideas:

For a different look, instead of adhering a decorated plastic lens with the concave side up, try displaying it with the convex side up. If the glue dries completely clear, the charm and glitter will show through.

To save a step, try using squeezable "glitter glue."

Accommodate larger charms and other items by using baby food jar lids.

Replace charms with tiny toys for baby or child-themed projects.

Spell words and titles using a dimensional letter in each lens.

Add a back to a tiny frame so that it may be used in place of lenses or lids.

Stuff a bottle cap with mini dice and seed beads to decorate the lid of your own little fortune box.

Fashion a little folder of wedding wishes and adorn the cover with a bejeweled heart charm surrounded by micro beads.

LIVE LONG...LAUGH OFTEN LOVE MUCH

LIFE IS AN ADVENTURE SHARE IT WITH THOSE YOU LOVE

YOU WILL HAVE A LONG AND HAPPY MARRIAGE

Here's how to create the embellishments:

1 On the inside of the lens or cap, apply clear-drying wet glue directly from the bottle or with a small brush, evenly coating the entire inside surface.

2 Allow the glue to begin to set for a few moments, then carefully center and place the charm.

3 Sprinkle glitter, fine confetti, tiny glass beads or seed beads over the lens and charm onto the exposed glue. Note: If the charm you're using has a hole in the center, like the heart on the wedding folder, carefully apply two colors of beads. Let the glue dry completely overnight, then shake off the excess glitter or beads. If some are still clinging to the charm, use a dry paintbrush to brush them off. To finish, adhere rhinestones or other accents if desired.

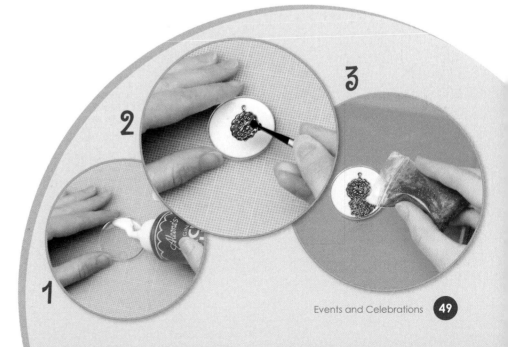

FASHION FAVORS

Combine treats with photo packaging for party favors

Celebrate a 50th wedding anniversary with a beautiful photo and chocolate coins.

An image from the wedding invitation is used to package small favors of birdseed to be opened and tossed in honor of the newlyweds.

Supplies:
Cellophane or plastic food bags
Photos or images printed on cardstock
Wording
Treats (candy, small toys, etc.)
Large stapler and staples
Dimensional accents (optional)
Scissors

With just a little extra effort you can create one-of-a-kind favors for the next event you host for less than you would spend purchasing premade ones. You can customize this project for any party or holiday by simply changing the photos and fillers to emphasize themes sophisticated and serious in nature, or fun and unabashedly silly. For an anniversary party, find a wedding photo to top a bag of chocolates. Fill birthday bags with favorite candy or stickers and toys. For weddings, there are always the standard mints, but get creative and think of something that truly represents the couple getting married. In addition to people, photos of objects such as flowers and clip art images also come in handy for this project. The possibilities for fashioning these fun party extras are practically endless.

To begin, use your computer and home printer to print the photo you are using onto heavyweight cardstock. You can also have color copies made professionally at a print shop, just make sure to indicate which kind of paper you prefer to have used. Also be sure to make the width of your photos the same width as the bags you plan on using. Next, cut around the image by either silhouetting the exact shape, or by simply cropping it into a rectangle or square. Fill the bags with treats or gifts, adding confetti or mylar shred for a decorative touch if desired. The quickest way to attach the photo headers onto the bags is to staple them, but they can also be taped or tied. You may also wish to adhere embellishments, labels or stickers to the headers and the bags. Make as few or as many as you need for the event, and don't be surprised if some guests resist opening their favors so they can keep them intact as cool keepsakes of the occasion.

A purchased tag is easily customized with a small photo and handwritten details.

More ideas:

Use computer software to type text directly on top of the photo before it's printed.

Try printing your photos and titles onto colored papers instead of plain white.

For really unique favors, use different photos on each one.

Use food bags with a zipper top so they can be easily opened and resealed by the guests.

In place of purchased plastic or cellophane bags, assemble your own in any size by folding and taping together flat cellophane.

Look for bags and cellophane in colors or printed with images.

For a small guest list, make a different favor suited for each individual.

Suggest to guests that they save their empty favor bag intact so that they can later insert a photo or other mementos of the party into it for a souvenir of the event.

Make a favor bag filled with items to be used at the party—such as name tags, noisemakers, confetti, game pieces, raffle tickets and the like.

Create favors that can serve as kits to be used during or after the event, such as "s'mores" ingredients for a camping theme or hangover remedies for the morning after a big bash.

Instead of bags, attach the photos and/or labels directly to small boxes or tins.

In addition to small favors, create one-of-a-kind gifts by designing custom packaging for large items such as wine bottles.

Get friends or family members to help you put together the favors assembly-line style—you could even make a party of it.

Small cloth bags can be used too. Here a photo of the couple is attached with an embellished safety pin for a pretty engagement-party favor.

Instead of a photo, create a decorative title to top a bag filled with a custom-made CD and themed trinkets.

For fun kids favors, adorn a small bag of jellybeans with a photo and the age of the birthday girl.

Lordy, Lordy, look who's 40!

Attach a childhood photo of the guest of honor to a small bag of antacids for an "over the hill" themed party.

ARCHIVE AUTOGRAPHS

Create frames to showcase prized signature books

Supplies:
Black or white foam board, ¼" thick
Small purchased or
handmade album
Autographs (originals or copies)
Photos of people who signed
Printed papers
Wording and embellishments
Double-sided sheet adhesive
Cardstock
Mat board or chipboard
Metal-edged ruler
Craft knife

Have guests at a wedding sign in, leaving space for their photos to be added later.

In these days of e-mail and voice mail, a handwritten note or name seems like an endangered species. Save those specimens you've collected from special occasions and display them in a place where you can appreciate them anytime you please. Create a frame and blank album before an event to serve not only as a decoration, but as the station for all the guests to sign in. Be sure to designate spots on each page for photos to be added later. Whether it's for your own party or for a gift for the guest of honor, this project turns a time-honored tradition into a keepsake you can display. To showcase a collection of autographs from friends or celebrities, make copies of the originals and include them all together in one framed album. Place it in a prominent place such as a coffee table for a great conversation piece. You could even carry the small album with you for garnering new signatures while on the go. A few inexpensive materials are all you need to fashion these fun and functional exhibits.

More ideas:

Try wavy edged or circle frames in addition to square and rectangular frames.

For thicker albums, cut and adhere two pieces of foam board together to create a deeper window.

Use foil tape or border stickers to conceal the raw edges of the frame.

Cut more than one window in the frame to accommodate two or more books.

Attach a decorative band of paper or fiber over the window to help hold the album in place.

Attach two frames to stand like an open book and place an album in each window, each filled with regards from only one person, such as each parent of a new grad or new mother.

Apply a coat of decoupage medium or spray varnish as a protective finish for the paper-covered frame.

Note: If including original autographs, pay close attention to the archival quality of the material being used.

As a gift for a departing co-worker, pass a tiny album around the office for everyone to express his or her best wishes.

Contain a collection of celebrity autographs in a collaged frame.

Here's how to build the frame:

1 Use a metal-edged ruler and sharp craft knife to measure and cut a piece of foam board several inches larger than the album it will frame. When cutting, pass through the board at least twice to assure a smooth and complete separation of the pieces. Next, in the center of the foam board, measure and cut a window that is about ¼" larger than the album.

2 Use sheet adhesive to smoothly adhere printed paper to the front of the frame, trimming away all excess, including inside the window. Then, apply sheet adhesive to the back of the frame, trimming any excess, and adhere the cardstock. Trim the excess from around the outside of the frame, but leave the window intact.

3 Cut a triangle of chipboard measuring shorter than the frame. Along one side, score and fold a ¼" strip. Hold it against the back of the frame to check the angle that it will stand at and make adjustments as needed. Apply adhesive to the back of the thin strip and firmly adhere it to the back of the frame to create a stand. Finish the front of the frame by adding desired accents.

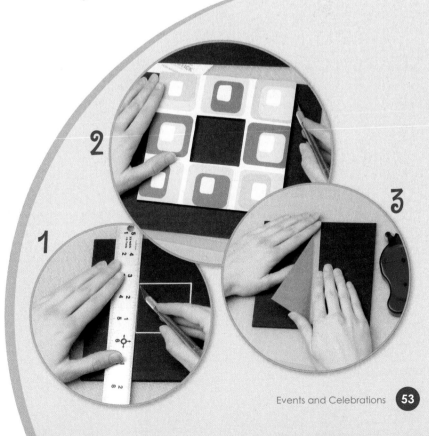

Chapter three

Babies and Children

SAVE SONOGRAMS

House ultrasound photos in pocket-sized books

Supplies:

Pocket-sized booklet
Printed papers
Baby-related image
Self-adhesive acrylic square
or flat glass pebble
Copies of sonogram photos
Double-sided sheet adhesive
Wording
Embellishments
Colored floss
Dry adhesive
Clear-drying glue (optional)
Cutting mat
Pen or pencil

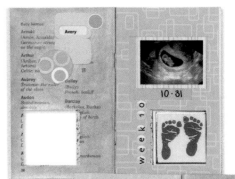

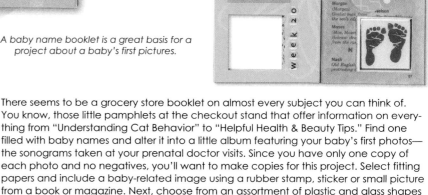

A baby name booklet is a great basis for a project about a baby's first pictures.

There seems to be a grocery store booklet on almost every subject you can think of. You know, those little pamphlets at the checkout stand that offer information on everything from "Understanding Cat Behavior" to "Helpful Health & Beauty Tips." Find one filled with baby names and alter it into a little album featuring your baby's first photos—the sonograms taken at your prenatal doctor visits. Since you have only one copy of each photo and no negatives, you'll want to make copies for this project. Select fitting papers and include a baby-related image using a rubber stamp, sticker or small picture from a book or magazine. Next, choose from an assortment of plastic and glass shapes sold as scrapbook embellishments to find one that's just larger than the image. Combine these elements as described in the steps to create a custom cover, then decorate the pages with paint glazes and printed papers, highlighting names you considered for your baby before he or she was born. The pages of these pamphlets are usually rather thin, so adhere some of them together for strength if desired. Add the sonogram photos and dates to finish this perfect addition to your baby book or box of mementos.

More ideas:

Add journaling to the pages describing what happened, including how you and your partner felt when you viewed the sonograms.

Incorporate other dimensional elements in the windows, such as large charms, silk flowers and dimensional letters spelling your baby's name.

Experiment with different shaped windows or even multiple windows on one cover.

Customize other grocery store booklets, which may include creating a birthday gift from a horoscope booklet, a pet album from a pet advice booklet, a dinner party invitation from a recipe booklet, etc.

Note: Since these mini booklets are likely not acid-free, spray them with an archival spray before beginning this project.

Add a mysterious question mark to the cover of a word-search booklet and hide the words "I'm Pregnant" inside for a fun way to announce the news to a loved one.

Here's how to create the cover:

1 Use sheet adhesive to adhere colorful paper smoothly over the front and back covers, trimming away the excess.

2 Place a clear self-adhesive acrylic square over the image and trim away the excess paper. Place the piece on the cover in the desired location and trace around it. If the clear shape you are using is not self-adhesive, use a clear adhesive to glue it over the image.

3 Cut the window by slipping a self-healing cutting mat or thick piece of chipboard between the last page of the pamphlet and its back cover. Clipping all the pages together helps to keep them from slipping as you cut. Use a craft knife with a fresh new blade and a metal-edged ruler to cut along the lines on the cover. Press firmly, but don't expect to make it through all the pages on one or two passes. Take your time and cut each line several times.

4 Remove the pieces as they become free, repeating cuts when necessary. Once all the pieces are cut away, adhere the embellishment to the inside of the back cover, centering it in the window. To finish, decorate the window with a thin frame of paper and tie the album shut with floss.

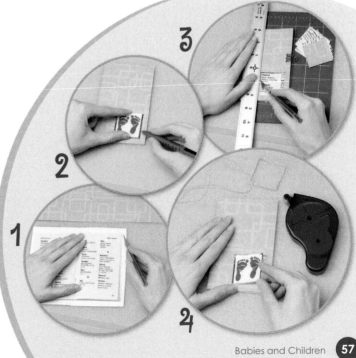

TRACK TIME

Create custom titles for baby albums using wood shapes

Month-by-month photos recollect a growing belly.

Supplies:

Blank album
Photos of you or your child
Printed papers
Wording and accents
Wooden craft shapes
Letter patterns or template
Pigment inkpad
Acrylic paint
Heat tool
Small paintbrush
Sandpaper
Pencil (#2 or softer)
Glue

During pregnancy it seems like the baby will never arrive, but before you know it the little one is here and his or her first years seem to pass even faster. These quick little albums are a perfect way to help record those fleeting moments before they are gone forever. Make an album documenting your pregnancy with photos and notes from each month. After the birth, take a photo of your baby each week or month for a scrapbook documenting his or her first year. You may also wish to build a book of your child's handprints as he or she grows, or create an album all about special baby "firsts." Continue these special timelines as your child grows by making birthday or school albums that you can add to each year. Create a custom wood title for each album cover to clearly state the contents inside and you will have an irreplaceable chronicle of your child's early life.

Paint a second color over the first coat on the wood shapes to create multicolored titles.

More ideas:

In addition to squares and circles, use wooden hearts, stars and animals.

Use one larger wood shape for an entire title or use a separate one for each letter.

In place of creating your own carbon with pencil, use purchased transfer paper.

Experiment with different grits of sandpaper for varied sanding effects.

Try sanding in different patterns, such as straight up and down or in a circular pattern.

For custom embellishments, decorate wood shapes with patterns or designs in place of letters.

Use rubber stamps to apply the letters to the shapes.

For a baby's first-year album, take a photo of him or her with the same item each month, such as a stuffed animal (for scale) or a daily calendar page (to document the dates).

For each of your child's birthdays, photograph him or her in front of the same tree or object each year, or holding up a sign with his or her age.

Store these little timeline albums together in a cool box, complete with its own wood shape title bearing your child's name.

Try stamping a pattern onto the background of each painted shape to decorate the title for an album of your child's growing handprints.

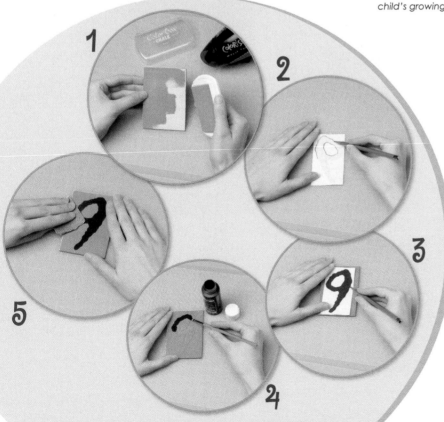

Here's how to create the wooden titles:

1 Use an inkpad to apply color directly to the front and sides of each wooden shape, then set the ink with a heat tool for 20 seconds. Note: You can also paint the shapes with acrylic paints.

2 Copy each figure onto paper to create a pattern, then carbon the back with pencil. If you can't see the image through the paper, place it over a window or light box.

3 Place the pattern right side up on top of the painted shape and use a pencil to trace around the outline, transferring the letter onto the wooden shape. Removable tape can be used to hold the pattern in place.

4 Use a small paintbrush to paint the figure onto the shape and allow it to dry completely.

5 Lightly sand the wood shape to give it a worn look.

ANNOUNCE ARRIVALS

Craft creative birth announcements with transparency sheets

A birth announcement should be as unique as the baby it is heralding. The versatility of using transparencies for handmade announcements makes it easy to accomplish just that. Transparency sheets can be found at office supply, craft and most scrapbooking stores and are often available in acid-free and archival versions unlike some acetates. Once primarily used for overhead projections, transparencies have become yet another supply that artists and crafters call upon for their projects. You can color, paint, print, stamp, emboss and cut transparencies as easily as paper. One fun and quick way to work with a clear sheet is to paint your own design on the back. Follow the steps shown here and decorate the shape with your baby's name, weight and birth date. Crop a photo into the same shape as the announcement, include it in the envelope and it's ready to be sent. Also look for transparency sheets in different colors or that come printed with images and designs. Cut them into pages, add Baby's photos and info and bind them with staples or jump rings. There are sheets made specifically for photocopying and printing onto with laser printers, presenting endless options for your own custom transparencies. Experiment with the other ideas listed here for making announcements as well as unique invitations, greeting cards and mini albums.

Paint a pretty flower for a baby girl's birth announcement. See page 94 for pattern.

ANGELINA rose

WELCOME
April 30, 2003
7lbs.11oz
19"-long

Supplies:
Clear or printed
transparency sheets
Photos of the newborn
Printed papers
Envelopes
Acrylic paints (optional)
Permanent markers (optional)
Alphabet stamps and solvent
inkpad (optional)
Staples or jump rings (optional)
Wording
Dry adhesive

More ideas:

Print a photo of your baby directly onto a sheet for a transparent portrait page in your announcement.

When stamping onto the transparency sheets, use quick-drying solvent ink for best results, as it won't smear as easily as pigment ink.

Purchase or make solid-colored transparency sheets and cut them into shapes to use as pages. For example, create duck shapes from yellow sheets, or stars from blue sheets.

Stamp or print designs onto the sheets, then add color accents with permanent markers.

Instead of using thin transparency sheets, try the painting technique on thicker acrylic pieces.

In addition to pages, use transparencies to create one-of-a-kind embellishments.

Try using transparency sheets in place of paper in many of your favorite paper crafting projects.

Make mini albums like these to include in a baby book or on your full-size scrapbook pages.

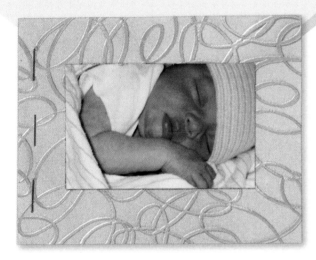

Transparencies preprinted with colorful designs are ready to cut and use for a little flip album announcement.

Stamp and wet emboss onto a piece of transparency and use it for the cover of a two-page announcement.

Here's how to reverse paint an image onto a transparent sheet:

1 To create the outline of your design, freehand draw, use a template or lay the transparency over a pattern or picture. Use waterproof permanent markers that are designed to write on slick surfaces. You can also use paint and a small brush for this step.

2 Paint over the design with acrylic paints. Use solid colors, or try loosely blending colors for an added effect. You can also experiment with thicker or thinner coats for variations in the opacity of the paint. After applying the paint, set the piece aside and allow it to dry completely.

3 Use a sharp craft knife or scissors to cut out the image. Turn the piece over and use it as is, or use clear sheet adhesive to adhere paper to the painted side, leaving a smooth shiny surface on top with your painting showing through. If desired, use permanent markers or stamps and solvent ink to add words to the smooth front side.

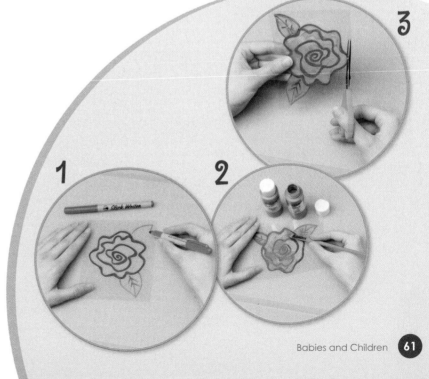

COLLECT CHARACTERS

Enhance albums featuring children's characters with tiny frames

Feature photos from your own childhood, even if they are a little embarrassing.

Supplies:

Small album or blank book
Inkable frame embellishment or small dimensional frame
Transparency or clear plastic sheet
Photos of children with characters
Stamps or images of faces or characters
Printed papers and wording
Small dimensional items and other accents
Permanent markers or ink
Clear-drying glue
Dimensional adhesive dots
Metal-edged ruler

There are plenty of opportunities to meet children's "celebrities" and to snap photos of your kids with them. There's Santa and the Easter Bunny at the mall, cartoon and storybook characters at amusement parks, theme restaurants and special events, team mascots after games and clowns and magicians at parties. They don't even have to be "real." Look for figures and statues of your children's favorite characters for fun photo opportunities. Make one album for all of the photos, make separate books for each holiday season or craft individual albums for each trip and event. Additionally, look through your own childhood pictures to create a book of your own encounters with kids' characters. Include any ticket stubs or autographs you may have and add journaling with the date, place and a short description of the child's reaction. Build a miniature shadow box like the ones shown here, capturing a funny face in a little picture frame, faux negative or even a tiny TV screen covered in "glass." They're the perfect way to finish off a book that will bring smiles for years to come.

Try using different frames for this project, such as small metal, wood or paper frames.

Include small loose items such as beads, confetti or glitter inside the enclosed frames for fun shaker boxes.

Cut the thin plastic from product packaging for a free source of "glass."

Try using colored plastic or even plastic printed with images for the "glass."

For unique titles or greetings, place dimensional lettering inside the frames.

Incorporate these little frames into fun cards, magnets and jewelry.

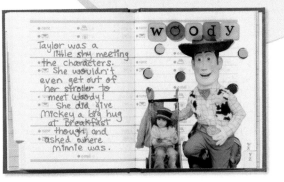

Fill an album with photos of kids and kids-at-heart meeting characters on a family trip to a theme park.

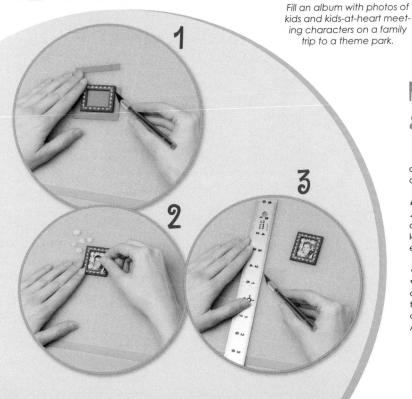

Here's how to assemble the frames:

1 Colorize an inkable frame embellishment with permanent markers or stamping ink. Note: You will need to set stamping ink with a heat tool. Adhere cardstock to the back of the frame and trim away the excess.

2 Adhere items inside the frame. Dimensional items may be used if they are no thicker than the frame. Apply dimensional adhesive dots to small photos or paper images at different levels. Be sure to leave a tiny amount of space between the items and the inside edges of the frame.

3 To cover the frame with "glass," measure and cut a piece of clear plastic that is the size of the frame opening, plus 1/8" longer on two sides. Use a craft knife to lightly score the two 1/8" edges, then fold them both down. Apply small amounts of clear-drying glue along the two 1/8" edges, then tuck the plastic inside the frame. Allow to dry, then adhere directly to your project.

MAINTAIN MEMENTOS

Stuff photo sleeves full of childhood mementos

The sentimental value of childhood mementos makes them seem too priceless to part with, but there comes a point when it's just not sensible to keep everything. It's easy to accumulate boxes and boxes of beloved baby clothes, musty stuffed animals and piles of papers until you have to give up your parking space in the garage to accommodate them!

As an alternative to that scenario, start taking photos or scans of large items, and keep only originals that are small enough to store within small albums. Next, begin compiling quick albums that are organized by theme. For example, each year create a small book for your child's birthday filled with small party mementos. Cut scraps from the wrapping paper to use as backgrounds in your albums and save an invitation, a napkin and pieces of the party decorations to include. Then add photos, cards, gift tags and ribbon and incorporate lists of guests that attended and the gifts that were received. This project works perfectly for baby showers, too.

Go through baby clothes and save a precious few, then photograph favorites or make scans of details like cute prints and appliqués of those you intend to get rid of. If some items are too worn or stained to give away, cut actual swatches to include in the album. Whether they're pink and frilly or bright and bold, these fabric samples, in addition to photos of the baby wearing them, make wonderful albums. Similarly, instead of saving dozens of beloved toys, shoot photos of them while being held by their owners. For instance, take a picture of an old teddy bear when you finally part ways to compare it to how it looked when brand new. Whether they are mementos and memories from your own childhood or those of your children, this project is a great and compact way to preserve them for generations to come.

Supplies:
4 x 6" photo album
Photos and/or scans of mementos
Mementos
Printed papers
Wording
Stickers and other embellishments

Little samples of gift wrap and trimmings will help you remember the details of a special day.

Never forget favorite stuffed friends by making a little book dedicated just to them.

A small album is a much more practical way to save baby clothes than keeping them boxed in the garage.

More ideas:

This is also a great way to manage and organize all those other baby mementos like the wristband from the hospital or locks from a first haircut.

Try this project as a compact means of archiving a child's art. Cut small pieces to include in an art album, or scan favorites and print them at a reduced size, always making sure to add the date and age they were created.

Make a book for adding each year's report card and school photo.

Try this project for preserving an adult's mementos too, like those from milestone parties and other special outings and events.

PRESERVE PORTRAITS

Tuck tiny portraits into hand-decorated matchboxes

Regardless of their era, school pictures are a great way to show a child growing up.

Supplies:

Empty matchbox
Small purchased or handmade album
Printed papers
Professional or personal portraits of kids
Stickers and other embellishments
Wording
Small dimensional items
Clear dimensional glaze
Double-sided sheet adhesive
Glue

Yearly portraits of children are not only a great way to track physical growth, but changing fashions and styles as well. Just think, in 15 years your kids' hairstyles and clothes will look as dated as your childhood photos look to them now. Whether you use professional portraits or ones you took yourself each year, this project is a great way to organize photos chronologically and turn them into fun heirlooms at the same time. Follow the steps shown to decorate a matchbox, then fill it with a tiny hand-crafted album. Make a small book by folding papers and stapling them together at the spine, or create accordion pages that fold directly out of the matchbox. Add school portraits and the grade year to the pages, or include favorite personal photos and the date they were taken. If your child is still young, make enough blank pages to add photos each year until he or she graduates. Complete the album with any embellishments you like and tuck it inside the matchbox for a fun little timeline that can be enjoyed anywhere, anytime.

Use a larger kitchen matchbox to store a collection of classmates' loose school pictures.

Use beads and charms to adorn a box of pretty portraits.

More ideas:

Create a matchbox to contain the school pictures of friends. Your children could take it on the last day of school and add in his or her classmates' summer phone numbers and e-mail addresses.

Create a box for a special teacher gift. Fill it with a photo and note from each student and include the school year and grade on the cover.

For instant organization, stack the photos in order, tie a ribbon around them and simply place them inside.

For an added touch, sprinkle glitter onto the glaze before it dries.

Instead of covering a plain matchbox with paper, use paint or stamps and ink to decorate the outside.

For a more substantial glaze, apply another coat for thickness.

Use this technique to decorate the lids of tins or the covers of small albums.

Try this project using your yearly family portraits as well.

Include a photo on the lid decoration, then fill the box with tiny mementos in place of an album.

Here's how to decorate the matchbox covers:

1 Cover a real matchbox or a blank one sold for crafting with printed paper by cutting a strip that measures the same width as the matchbox lid. Wrap the lid completely and trim any excess length. Use sheet adhesive to adhere the paper to assure the smoothest, most complete bond. If desired, measure and cut a matching piece of paper to line the inside of the matchbox.

2 Decorate the cover by gathering small trinkets or mementos and adhering them with small amounts of wet glue to completely cover the lid, then allow the glue to dry.

3 Apply a generous coating of dimensional glaze directly from the bottle. Be sure to read the specific instructions for the brand being used. The glaze will most likely look milky until it is completely dry, at which point it will become hard and crystal clear.

GIVE GAMES

Decoupage dimensional surfaces for fun children's games

Babies can build with these blocks or fit them together to see their friends' smiling faces.

Supplies:

Wooden, plastic or metal shapes
Photos of family and friends
Printed papers
Alphabet stickers
Sheet adhesive
Decoupage medium
Small flat paintbrush
Craft Knife and scissors
Ruler
Pencil

Babies and small children love to look at photos of faces, especially ones they know. Instead of just placing these photos in an album, turn them into games that are not only fun to play, but that make great room decorations, too. Make simple puzzle blocks that can be placed together to form photos of your child's favorite playmates. When not being played with, they look especially cute perched up on a shelf in the nursery. For older children, make the puzzles even more challenging by using different papers on each block behind a face, instead of using matching pieces like on the blocks shown here.

Make your own memory games by covering one side of a handful of identical shapes with the same paper, and matching pairs of decoupaged photos on the other sides. To play, lay the shapes with the identical sides up and turn them over two at a time, looking for two that have the same person on them. If a matched set isn't found, turn them back facedown and take another turn. When two matching faces are found, pick them up and continue looking for more. This game can be played alone or with others, and older kids can actually make the pieces themselves. The decoupage finish is quick and easy and makes the paper-covered pieces durable enough to be played with again and again and even gently washed. With babies and toddlers, only use these games with supervision, and if your child is still putting everything in his or her mouth, it's best to just use these as decorations until he or she is a little older and has more discriminating tastes.

More ideas:

Sand the edges and corners of covered wooden blocks for a worn, antiqued look.

Instead of using printed papers, simply paint the shapes before adhering the silhouetted photos.

For an even quicker project, omit the printed paper backgrounds and simply crop the photos to fit the shapes being used.

In addition to using alphabet stickers for wording, use rubber stamps or print out names with your computer.

Add texture to the finish on your project by applying the decoupage medium with choppy or swirled brush strokes.

Besides decoupage medium, finish and protect these projects by painting or spraying them with polyurethane or varnish.

For another type of puzzle, crop photos into simple shapes, adhere them to foam board and then use a sharp craft knife to cut them into puzzle pieces. These can then be fitted perfectly back together just like a traditional puzzle.

Make games that help your child learn numbers or the ABCs by using corresponding photos.

In addition to photos of people, take photos of toys or other objects your child sees every day to create games that teaches him or her words and spelling.

Create blocks or puzzles using only photos of one child for a great gift for his or her grandparent.

Turn recycled frozen juice can lids into a fun family memory game.

Here's how to create the puzzle blocks:

1 Choose a photo and a different printed paper for each side of the puzzle, totaling six. One side at a time, adhere double-sided sheet adhesive and trim away the extra with a craft knife.

2 Cut a piece of paper that is slightly larger than all four cubes. Next, peel the backing off of the sheet adhesive on one of the blocks and lay it sticky-side-down to adhere the paper to the cube. Use a craft knife to carefully cut through the paper around the exact shape of the block. Put the covered block back in place with the other three and continue adhering and trimming them, making sure they are in the same order to ensure that the pattern on the printed paper will match up on the four sides.

3 Continue the aforementioned steps until all sides of the four blocks are covered with paper. Next, silhouette the photos with scissors and lay them one at a time over a desired side of the puzzle. Find a placement for the photo that will not cut through an important feature such as an eye and use a sharp pencil to make a tiny tick mark where each block meets behind the photo. Use a ruler and craft knife to quarter the photo according to the four marks. Use sheet adhesive to smoothly adhere each portion of the face onto each of the four blocks. Add alphabet stickers for initials or names. Repeat this step for applying the other five photos onto each side of the puzzle.

4 Use a flat paintbrush to apply decoupage medium to each block according to the manufacturer's instructions. Allow the blocks to dry completely before applying additional coats.

Chapter four

Home and Holidays

CAPTURE COLLECTIONS

Feature your favorite collectibles in fabric books

Supplies:
Oilcloth or fabric and iron-on vinyl
Photos of collections
Wording
Embellishments
Fibers or jump rings
Double-sided sheet adhesive
Metal-edged ruler
Iron
Craft knife and scissors
1/8" hole punch

These fabrics are simply perfect for a salt and pepper shaker collection.

Even if you can't sew, it's easy to incorporate cloth into your memory crafts. And with fabric available in so many great prints and patterns, it would be a shame not to. Oilcloth, the old-fashioned waterproof fabric used mainly to make tablecloths, is perfect for making little album pages. It's durable, the ends don't fray when cut, it's "punchable" and it's easy to adhere together with dry adhesives. Look for vintage pieces, find new and reproduction versions at large fabric stores or use the steps shown here to create your own oilcloth. The binding ideas shown here also allow more pages to be easily added to your book at any time.

These sturdy fabric pages would be great for albums about many different themes, but they are especially fitting for books about special collections. From silly retro knick-knacks to beautiful Native American pottery, you are sure to find fitting fabrics for any type and style of collectible. Take photos of your prized possessions and add the location, date and price of purchase for future reference, both to track value and to avoid duplicate purchases when adding to your collection. These albums are durable enough to be carried shopping, to take to conventions and trade shows, or to simply show off your collection away from home. If you collect small and flat items such as vintage greeting cards, old luggage labels or dried flowers, create an album that will hold and protect the original collection itself. Adhere clear acid-free pockets to contain the items in your book and you will have an album that not only displays your collection, but that also protects and preserves it.

Protect original pieces by placing them in acid-free envelopes before adding them to the album.

More ideas:

Put photos and other flat embellishments under the vinyl before ironing it onto the cloth.

Sprinkle glitter or sequins on top of the fabric before ironing on the vinyl.

Instead of using solid fabric swatches, lay down several small pieces to create a patchwork held together by the applied vinyl.

Just punch one hole in the corner of each page and use a binder ring to attach them together key chain-style.

In addition to iron-on vinyl, laminating sheets can work for this project as well.

Make a record of the décor of a room in your house by using samples of the fabrics for pages, adding photos of furniture and accents. Carry it with you when shopping to easily match new finds.

Include actual register receipts on your pages for irrefutable proof of your collectible's purchase price, date and place, making your album useful for insurance purposes.

Colorful oilcloth is perfect for pages featuring a collection of funky fruit plaques.

Here's how to make your own oilcloth album pages:

1 Pick out one or more fabrics that match the color scheme and theme of your collection and roughly cut out squares or rectangles slightly larger than you would like your book's pages to be. Unroll the iron-on vinyl and cut the same size and number of pieces.

2 Peel the backing off of the vinyl pieces one at a time and hand-smooth them over the cloth swatches. Lay the backing on top and use a heated iron to permanently adhere the vinyl to the fabric according to the manufacturer's instructions.

3 Allow the swatches to cool, then cut pieces of sheet adhesive the same size as the swatches. You will need half as many pieces of sheet adhesive as cloth swatches. Peel one side of the backing off of the adhesive and apply it to the back of one swatch. Remove the remaining backing and adhere the back of another swatch on top of the exposed adhesive.

4 Use a craft knife and metal-edged ruler to measure and trim away the rough edges, creating pages that are all exactly the same size. Use a hole punch to make several holes along one side of each page and then use cord, ribbon or metal jump rings to bind them together.

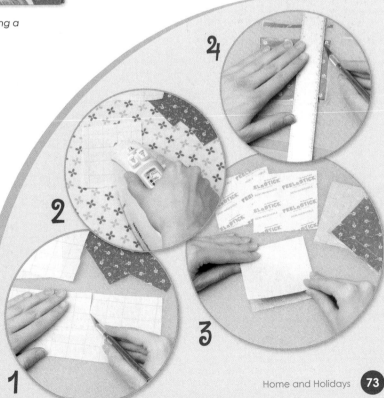

KEEP KEYS

Fashion one-of-a-kind key chains from favorite photos

Create a collage using a favorite vacation photo and stickers to fill a purchased photo key chain.

With an attached photo of the owner, you'll never forget whose spare keys are whose!

Supplies:

Photo key chains, key tags or other tags
Bead chain or metal rings
Photos of loved ones
Printed papers
Stickers and other embellishments
Sheet laminate, paper glaze or clear embossing ink and powder

Although there are thousands of key chains you can readily buy, their mass-produced nature can't speak to your personality and what's important to you quite the way customized photo key chains can. Make a practical item pretty and never again be caught without family photos to show people you run into or meet. For fun options, attach a tag to each key you use with a photo of what it's for, or identify a spare key to a friend's place by adding his or her photo to it. Create a key chain with both artistic flair and functionality that's actually a little embellishment or keepsake album. You always have your keys with you, so turn them into something you'll love to look at every day to help cheer you up the next time you're stuck in traffic or a long line at the store.

Hardware and home improvement stores have fairly large selections of photo key chains and keys tags in addition to colored rings and clasps. In addition there are many metal and plastic tags sold for scrapbooking that are durable enough to serve as key chains. Keep an eye out for mini books and journals with attached rings, often sold to decorate children's backpacks, as well as found items such as bottle caps and slide mounts. To decorate a plastic photo key tag, simply create a small collage, cut it to size and slip it into the sleeve. For solid tags, you'll have to adhere your papers, photos and stickers directly to their surfaces. Use sheet adhesive to do this, since the entire back surface of the element needs to be smoothly adhered.

For a protective coating on key chains without sleeves, apply one of many waterproof coatings sold for craft or furniture projects, or try the wet embossing technique in the "Magnetize Memories" project on page 30. For the quickest, least messy option, simply cut laminating sheets, available at craft and office supply stores, to size to cover your art and make it durable enough to carry in your purse. To finish the pieces, add desired dimensional elements such as rhinestones using a very strong glue to assure they stay affixed.

Adhere printed papers and a photo of your husband to a discarded countertop sample chip, adding a protective coating of clear embossing powder.

More ideas:

Use purchased photo key tags to create key chains you can easily change whenever you'd like.

Recall that cool car you used to have by anchoring a spare key to a customized key chain.

Add a collage key chain to one of your old house keys so you never forget what it was for.

Easily identify keys you don't carry with you every day, like those to the padlock on the storage shed or your locker at the gym with colorful, customized tags.

Create protective finishes on your pieces with transparency sheets or self-adhesive acrylic shapes.

Add beads and charms to your chains for an artistic touch.

Use handy photo key tags to create cool necklaces and pins.

Incorporate photos or images of flowers and other objects for quick and fun favors and gifts.

Feature humorous or inspirational quotes on key chains.

Make an eye-catching key chain by adhering metallic diamond-plate paper behind a sturdy acrylic frame.

Fill plastic key tags with photos and initials of your kids for a portable family album.

Add a title and tiny pictures to a cute key chain journal for a brag book you'll always have with you.

Give your cat glasses for a key chain that will always make you a smile.

Turn a vintage family key into a keepsake by adding photos of the house and its occupants.

SHAKE SNOW

Slip images of home inside snow globes

Supplies:
Photo snow dome
Photos of houses
Decorative images
Dimensional paints
Small dimensional accents
Glue and dimensional adhesive

Change the weather whenever you'd like with a snow dome that's wintertime on one side and summertime on the other. Craft a cozy snow dome featuring wintry photos of your home.

There's something magical about shaking a snow dome and watching the glittery contents slowly float and settle around the scene inside. You can move your own home into just such a wintry world by purchasing a photo snow dome you can customize at a hobby or discount store. The bottoms of these domes open easily, revealing a slot to accommodate your own photos. You'll have approximately ¼" to work with, making it possible to slip in charms, buttons and other thin items and also to adhere images in a second layer using dimensional adhesive. Once the art is inside the dome, the view through the water exaggerates the depth, adding even more dimension.

Choose a clear photo of the house you currently live in or one you want to remember, such as the house you grew up in. Reduce the photo so it that it fits inside your snow dome. Use the template that comes with the dome to measure and cut the photo to the exact shape, or use it to cut background paper. Silhouette cut the photo of the house. If desired, cut details of the house from a second print and adhere them with dimensional adhesive over the full photo. Decide what type of world you'd like the house to reside in and get creative. Use dimensional paints and glitter glues to accentuate a photo of your house in the winter. Back it with images from vintage greeting cards and add tiny snowflakes and a snowman to complete the wintry environment. Or, move your home to outer space, the beach or any other place in your imagination. To finish, glue rhinestones or other embellishments to the outside of the dome and choose the perfect place in your real home to put your scene on display.

More ideas:

Before adhering the dimensional items to the art, make sure they will fit inside the snow dome by slipping them inside and then sliding them out.

Include silhouette-cut portraits of the house's occupants.

Create additional art for the other side of your dome, add a fun saying or even include its address and location.

Build snow domes that double as holiday decorations by showing the front of your house all decked out for Halloween or Christmas.

Honor your heritage by building a snow dome around a vintage photo of a family home.

Revisit all the homes you have lived in by creating a special snow dome for each.

Make separate snow domes showing your house in each of the four seasons.

For a great housewarming gift, take a shot of your friend's new abode and decorate it for it's own custom snow dome.

If you don't live in a house, craft a snow dome with a photo of your apartment's or condo's front door, balcony or window.

For other great snow dome themes, use photos from winter sports, snowstorms, snowman building or snowball fights.

For a fun "Naughty or Nice" snow dome, put a photo of your child smiling on one side and frowning or crying on the other.

Create your own custom vacation souvenirs by enclosing photos and other mementos from your trip.

Accentuate the beauty of your home's garden by adding dimensional flowers and butterflies.

Fashion a small shuttered window for your house and surround it with tiny objects that define how you feel about your home.

Send your home out of this world by placing it in front of a photo of the moon and shiny star stickers.

Make a fun retro setting for an ultramodern home.

PRESENT PUMPKINS

Use paper brads to bind expandable Halloween albums

Whether creepy or cute, nothing says "Halloween" like a grinning jack-o'-lantern.

Supplies:
Colored or printed cardstock
Photos of jack-o'-lanterns
Wording
Embellishments
$\frac{1}{8}$" hole punch
Paper fasteners or brads

The one-of-a-kind look of hand-carved jack-o'-lanterns is something you'll want to remember years after the spooky masterpieces were created. If your family carves pumpkins each year, be sure to photograph them and use the photos to make an album to serve as both a keepsake and a holiday decoration. Add a page or two featuring your family's creations every Halloween, or make each carver his or her own album to add pages and photos to each year. If you have children, won't it be fun to see how their carving skills improve every year?

It's very quick and simple to make these albums. Begin by selecting colored or printed cardstock, or by decorating plain sheets with markers, paint or stamps. Cut the sheets into little pages and bind them as described in the step-by-step photos. Pages can be decorated while they are in the album, but you may wish to disassemble, add photos and accents and then reassemble them. Embellishing the fronts of the brads with a letter makes for a fun decorative touch. When opened, these little albums make excellent "banners" to display during the Halloween season. Once you're ready to close and store them, just twist and turn the pages until they form a stack with the cover on top.

More ideas:

Instead of photographing the jack-o'-lanterns alone, capture the carvers holding their creations.

Look for brads and paper fasteners available in many colors and fun shapes.

Strengthen sheets of printed paper by adhering them to cardstock prior to cutting the shaped pages.

Instead of pumpkins, build a book with photos featuring each guest at your costume party.

Adorn the fronts of the brads with rhinestones or other small embellishments.

Experiment with other symmetrical page shapes such as diamonds or six-pointed stars.

For a fun banner, decorate the pages with letters spelling out "Happy Halloween" or "Trick or Treat."

Customize this project for a Christmas "garland" for your holiday mantel.

Try this binding technique for a fun way to display postcards or as a great way to create unique invitations and greeting cards for any occasion.

Here's how to build the albums:

1 Use a circle cutter to cut several small circles out of cardstock, or use a template or pattern to trace and cut rectangles, squares and other shapes. For a variation, make oblong pages or pages in slightly different sizes.

2 Using a hole punch that is just larger than the prongs on the brads, punch two holes centered on both sides of one page. Leave at least $1/8$" between the holes and the edge of the cardstock. Use the first punched page as a guide for placing the holes on the pages to follow. Punch one hole on the front and back pages and two holes on all the others.

3 To attach the pages, insert a brad through a hole on one page, then through another page. Bend the two prongs of the brad flat against the back. Continue adding pages until you have the desired number, or add a hole and a page to the book each year.

Colorful circles decorated with rolling stamps make perfect pages for your pumpkins.

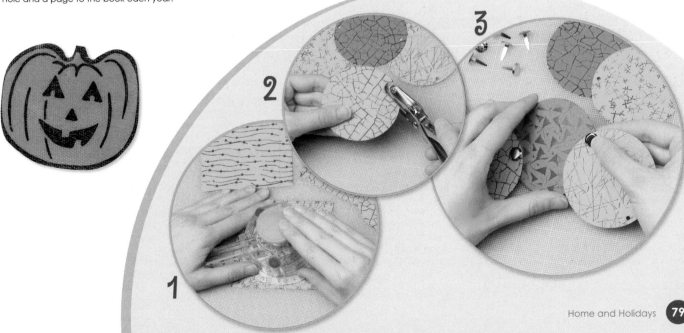

GIVE GRATITUDE

Fashion place cards for your Thanksgiving table with acrylic squares and foil tape

No one will wonder where to sit with these photo place cards.

No need to get out a glass cutter and safety goggles for this project! Plastic squares and self-adhesive foil tape are all you need to achieve the look of soldered glass for unique place cards, table decorations and favors. These place cards are surprisingly quick to create. Purchase acrylic crafting squares and foil tape from a craft and hobby store or online. The tape is available in silver and copper finishes and is made for soldering onto stained-glass projects. However, since it is self-adhesive, you can omit the soldering step and it's perfect for use on all kinds of paper crafts. To assemble the standing cards, follow the steps shown and adhere photos or Thanksgiving images to each. Adhere the pieces on the fronts and/or backs of the squares, using a clear sheet adhesive to assure complete adhesion and a clear view through the acrylic. Add the names of each guest and also the date and location of the dinner. For added meaning, leave a blank spot on each place card where friends and family can write what they are most thankful for. Create a new Thanksgiving tradition by having everyone take turns reading his or hers aloud. With these easy steps, you can create pieces that serve as place cards, decorations, keepsakes and even an activity!

Shoot a pretty seasonal photo for the front of each place card.

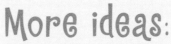

More ideas:

Customize these place cards to complement any party theme.

Incorporate glass microscope slides, small mirrors or even wood shapes in place of plastic squares.

Stamp and/or wet emboss words and images directly onto the acrylic.

Paint onto the acrylic to get the look of stained glass.

Use permanent markers on the silver foil tape to customize its color.

Adhere dimensional buttons or charms to the front of the place cards.

Bind more than two squares together to make a mini album.

Create unique jewelry, magnets or even wall art utilizing this technique.

Find fitting die cuts or stickers to adorn the place cards in place of photos.

Vintage or reproduction holiday images look nice too.

Create place cards or decorations that display your traditional table blessing.

Here's how to build the place cards:

1 Cut a length of tape slightly longer than needed to wrap around the square. At one end, center an edge of the square onto the adhesive side of the tape.

2 Wrap tape around the edges and press firmly with your fingers.

3 Wrap the tape around the corner and continue the previous step to cover all four sides of the square. Use a sharp craft knife to carefully trim away the excess tape.

4 Completely wrap the edges of two squares with the foil tape, then attach them together by stacking them and pressing a piece of the tape along one side. Use a craft knife to trim away any excess. Now the place card can be opened and stood up like a book or tent.

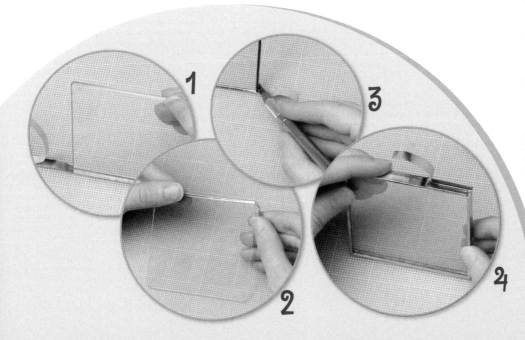

TREASURE TRADITIONS

Contain family traditions in decorative tins and boxes

In a star-shaped box, spell out your traditions for holidays and other special events. See page 94 for patterns.

We Make all of our HALLOWEEN Costumes from scratch!

Every Valentine's Day we make cookies for Daddy to take to everyone at work

For Mother's Day, Mommy always get breakfast in bed and a big Bouquet of Gerbera Daisies. Plus, we let her sleep in

HAPPY HOLIDAYS

Every Year for Nate's Birthday we go out for a big Italian dinner and to a movie of his choosing

DURING Thanksgiving we make and donate food baskets for the needy

On New Year's Eve we always Make fondue & stay up all night

Better wear green on Saint Patricks Day or GrandPa will pinch you!

One of our Christmas traditions is to hand make new ornaments for our holiday tree.

Supplies:

Small metal, wood or cardboard box with lid
Photos of family participating in traditions
Colored cardstock and printed papers
Inks, pens and paints
Rubber stamps (optional)
Wording
Assorted embellishments
Wet and dry adhesives

Every family has special traditions they follow and teach to their children. Whether they are religious in nature or silly and fun, traditions should be recorded so that they will always be remembered. Sure, you could just write them down, but this project allows you to not only document traditions, but to turn them into cherished heirlooms as well. To start, pick a theme and decorate a small container inside and out. Next buy or make a little album or assemble loose pages to fit inside, and add a title, journaling and photographs. Keeping these pieces small in scale makes it easy to create them in multiples. You may wish to make several in different themes for yourself and for family members. These little tokens make wonderful and meaningful gifts, especially for life's milestones, which may include your children moving out on their own, getting married or having their own children. Create one piece that covers all of your time-honored traditions or make separate ones for each holiday. These tradition boxes look great on display in the house. Place them on tabletops and mantels for easily accessible decorations. Add more pages each year with new photos of old traditions in action or to explain new traditions. Moreover, adding to your boxes each year can become a new family tradition itself!

More ideas:

Include favorite recipes, music, family jokes and stories in these little archives.

Look for premade albums that fit inside your chosen container.

In place of an album, fill your tin with tiny envelopes, each one containing a treasured family tradition.

Make it a family affair by having each family member list his or her favorite traditions.

Build accordion pages to extend from the container when it is opened.

Craft a separate project for each holiday and decorate a large container to store them in addition to other pieces of related memorabilia.

Present these tins and boxes as interactive gifts by designating each page with a holiday while leaving room for recipients to add their own journaling and photos.

Build a "tradition kit" by enclosing a description of the custom and the materials needed to carry it out, such as the parts for decorating a snowman or the ingredients for a special craft or recipe, then give it as a gift for someone far away to make him or her feel a little closer to home.

Note: If you would like your project to be passed from generation to generation, be mindful of the archival quality of all the materials you use.

Record all of the romantic traditions you partake in with your mate.

Paint and decorate a candy tin to create a fun container.

List the lyrics of lullabies you sang to your children so they can share them with their own.

Adorn a tin to honor your family's Hanukkah customs.

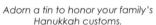

Cut loose pages to fit a tin, adding traditions on one side and photos on the other.

Build a little book in a box and list your family's Christmas traditions.

CREATE COUNTDOWNS

Craft calendars that conceal images beneath a scratch-off coating

Supplies:
Peel-and-stick
scratch-off paper
Small album or blank cards
Holiday photos
Printed papers
Wording
Fibers and accents
Permanent marker or
solvent ink pad
Rubber stamps (optional)

Decorate this year's album with photos from last year to be surprised by how much your family has changed.

Holiday advent calendars are especially fun for children, and this project allows you to create custom ones that adults can enjoy as well and that are beautiful enough to be displayed with other festive holiday decorations. Peel-and-stick paper with a scratch-away surface is a playful way to hide surprises under each date. Additionally, it is easy to use and is available in many colors. Use it to cover favorite holiday photos and activities that can be revealed on their designated day with the quick rub of a coin. Honor the eight nights of Hanukkah, countdown the 12 days of Christmas, celebrate New Year's Eve or even create a calendar for the whole month of December. Build the calendars in small albums or on standing cards, either for your own family or to send to others as unique gifts. This is also a perfect project for party favors. For a New Year's party, hide activities for partygoers to reveal and perform during the night. Include a photo of who to kiss at midnight, making sure to choose each person's mate. Or, play matchmaker and unite two single guests! Even after these little calendars and countdowns are used, they double as wonderful keepsakes of the holiday season.

Customize an advent calendar for the eight nights of Hanukkah.

More ideas:

Attach a coin or charm directly to the calendar for a ready-to-use scratching utensil.

Add an arrow and the words "Scratch Here" as instructions for others to follow.

Simplify your design for making many identical pieces, such as for party favors. Use a computer to duplicate and print all of the wording and photos and put the pieces together assembly line-style.

Incorporate a scratch-away surface for holiday gift tags and greeting cards.

Use this idea for other occasions too, such as calendars counting down the weeks to graduation, retirement or the due date of a pregnancy.

Experiment with printed papers and other images to create one-of-a-kind embellishments and decorations.

There are many other uses for the scratch-away paper, such as lottery tickets, games and charts. See the product packaging for even more ideas to try.

Create a fun New Year's Eve party favor that lists an activity for each hour of the evening.

The identity of a gift giver is revealed when the recipient rubs away the coating on a custom gift tag.

Here's how to use the scratch-off surface:

1 Crop to size the image to be hidden, then cut a slightly larger piece of the scratch-off paper. Peel the backing from the scratch-off paper and adhere it smoothly over the image. Trim the excess so it is the exact same shape and size as the cropped image.

2 Apply adhesive to the back of the covered image and adhere it to your project. Use a permanent marker or rubber stamps and solvent ink to add designs or wording to the surface.

3 To reveal the image beneath the surface, scratch away the coating with a coin or other small, sturdy item.

FORETELL FUTURES

Combine predictions and playing cards for a New Year's activity and keepsake

Will these two really keep their promises to exercise?

Supplies:

Game or playing cards
Binding punch and discs
Blank tags, labels or
slips of paper
Photos of New Year's
Eve celebrants
Printed papers
Decorative accents

For many, it's a New Year's Eve tradition to spend the evening playing games with family and friends. For a new addition to the night, use game cards and your imaginations to make small albums that list predictions and record resolutions for the upcoming year. To make it quick and fun at the party, assemble the album before or after New Year's Eve so that all that your guests will need to do is jot down their entries on tags or slips of paper you provide.

To make the albums, start by gathering game cards or playing cards. This is a great way to utilize misfit decks that are missing cards. Playing cards are very inexpensive to buy new and game cards can be found in board games at thrift stores and yard sales. Next, use a binding punch and binding discs to attach the card pages together, which are often available at office supply stores and at craft and scrapbooking stores. Once your book is bound, decorate the cover with the date and any other desired embellishments. On New Year's Eve, announce the activity to your guests and have everyone take a moment to write down his or her entry. This in itself will be entertaining, but the real fun comes next year when you bring out the finished album, reveal the past, revel in correct predictions and poke fun at forgotten resolutions.

More ideas:

At the party, put the blank tags or slips of paper in a big fishbowl or other fun container.

Supply self-adhesive labels for everyone's entry, then have guests pick the page and place their predictions into the albums themselves.

Be sure to take photos of all the participants to add to these little time capsules.

"Distress" the playing cards before binding them by painting, stamping or inking them.

For a family, make one album you can add a few pages to each year, or make each family member his or her own small book.

To keep your albums in a safe spot you won't forget, decorate a lidded box and add the words "Do not open until New Year's Eve."

Note: This technique is a great way to bind albums you may need to subtract or add pages to later.

Incorporate the kids' predictions in your album, or make them one of their own.

Decorate Loteria cards with glitter and rhinestones for a funky little album.

Be sure to include some New Year's Eve photos of the prediction-makers.

Here's how to bind the albums:

1 Decide how many pages the album will be and use a binding punch to punch holes down the left side of each card. Be sure to line them up the same way so that the punched shapes will be aligned on all of the cards.

2 One or two at a time, pop the cards onto the binding discs.

Note: A binding punch is a great investment, since it is such a quick, easy and attractive way to bind materials for craft projects, school projects, work projects and more.

Product Guide

Pages 8-9, Tools

Basic-Tweezers (Magic Scraps); paintbrushes (Winsor Newton); scoring tool (EK Success); clear ruler, bone folder (C-Thru Ruler); hammer (ScrapArts); pen (EK Success); permanent marker (Sanford)

Cutting-Scissors (EK Success); pinking shears (Fiskars); circle cutter (EK Success); craft knife (Hunt Corporation); cutting mat (Club Scrap); circle cutter (Fiskars); paper punch (EK Success)

Bonding-Dimensional adhesive (Ranger); dry adhesive applicator (EK Success); double-sided sheet adhesive (Therm O Web); glue pen (EK Success); wet glue (Duncan); super-strength glue (Aron Alpha); double-sided tape (Magic Scraps); pickup square (Therm O Web); adhesive dots (Glue Dots International)

Coloring-Ink pad (Clearsnap); color wash (Ranger); paint writer (Ranger); multisurface pen (Ranger); acrylic paints (Delta); colored pencil (Spectracolor); marker (Sakura); chalk (EK Success)

Stamping-Clear embossing pad (Stampabilities); flower, square, Happy Birthday, wavy line and multisquare stamps (Rubber Stampede); solvent ink pad (Tsukineko); mosaic stamp (Hampton Art Stamps); heart stamp (Stampendous!); embossing powder (Ranger)

Coating-Paper glaze (Ranger); de-acidifying spray (EK Success); paper glitter (Plaid); paper glitz (Scrapbook Diva); clear embossing powder (Ranger); decoupage medium (Plaid)

Binding-Thread (Coats & Clark); drill (Fiskars); hole punch (McGill); binding punch and discs (Rollabind); stapler (ACCO); foam pad (Scrapworks)

And More-Heat tool (EK Success); label maker (Dymo); cleanup tray (Tidy Crafts); ink applicator (Clearsnap); engraver (Magic Scraps); appliqué (Marvy)

Pages 10-11, Supplies

Albums-Brown (EK Success); pink (Bridgeport); blue (Kolo)

Containers-Round tin (Provo Craft); teal box (The Container Store); red box (found); brass box (vintage)

Papers-Blue texture (Paper Loft); pink dots (Doodlebug Design); black and white circles (KI Memories); vintage print (Paper Love Designs)

Ephemera-Vanilla label, postcard, hotel label (Me & My Big Ideas); ticket, tag, disc, card (found, vintage)

Die Cuts-Guitar, Hawaiian girl, purse (Meri Meri); flower pot (Colorbök); butterfly (ARTchix Studio); star (Paper Loft); square (KI Memories)

Lettering-Green E, purple G, blue A (Scrapbook Wizard); black K (Wordsworth);

orange M, purple U (Creative Imaginations); purple W, red ? (All My Memories); cherish, gold A (Stampendous!); blue T, orange F, green Y, X cube, E tile (found); smile (Scrapworks); S bead (Westrim); blue O (Foofala); green O, black C (KI Memories); heart H, girlfriends (Me & My Big Ideas); red B, aqua H, yellow M (Doodlebug Design); pink J, R tag, pink B (Karen Foster Design); 2 (ARTchix Studio)

Stickers-Film reel, glasses, pig, movie ticket, robot, record (Frances Meyer); orange flower, heart in square (Colorbök); atomic shape (Sassafras Lass); hibiscus flower, red heart (Creative Imaginations); button (Stampendous!); diamond (Gartner Studios); star, monkey, square (Mrs. Grossman's); pink dot, dog (EK Success); dotted circle (Doodlebug Design)

3D Accents-Flower square, buckle (KI Memories); yellow flower (Westrim); metal rose (ARTchix Studio); other accents (found, vintage)

Tags-Pink, blue, aqua, lime (Gartner Studios); 2 cream (DMD); copper, gold (Magic Scraps); silver (Scrap Ease)

Charms-Gold and copper space-age shapes (Magic Scraps); envelope, copper circle (ARTchix Studio); birdhouse, moon, dragonfly, cat, guitar, palm trees, Saturn (Boutique Trims); shoe (Blue Moon Beads); 3 stars (JHB International); other charms (found, vintage)

Frames-Paper orange, striped blue (KI Memories); brass circle, tiny rectangle (ARTchix Studio); slide mount (Loersch); circle sticker (All My Memories); silver rectangle (Scrapworks); label holder (Magic Scraps)

Buttons-Star, heart, leopard print, sparkly pink, face, teal, question mark, moon, hand (JHB International); other buttons (found, vintage)

Findings-Paper clips, binder clips, staples (Office Depot); silver bead chain (Magic Scraps); charm pin (Blue Moon Beads); safety pin, jump rings, wire, purple bead chain (Westrim); round clip (Scrapworks); pin back (ARTchix Studio)

Beads-(Blue Moon Beads)

Glitz-Rhinestones (Westrim); pipe cleaner (Fibre-Craft); glitter, shred (Magic Scraps); mirror (JewelCraft)

Fibers-Black and silver thread (Magic Scraps); striped, blue pompoms, pink, multicolored (Making Memories); purple (Scrapbook Wizard); green, red (Me & My Big Ideas); dots (Scrappy's); yellow (Wrights)

Metals-(Creative Impressions, Doodlebug Design, Emagination Craft, Jest Charming, Karen Foster Design, Keeping Memories Alive, Limited Edition Rubberstamps, Scrapworks)

And More-Oilcloth (source unknown); leopard print fabric (source unknown), pink and black envelope (Meri Meri); printed transparency (Magic Scraps)

Pages 12-13, Why Mini?

Postcards From Paradise-Album (DMD); paper, stickers (Creative Imaginations); stamp (Just For Fun Rubberstamps); title (Me & My Big Ideas)

Best Friends-Album (source unknown); stickers (Creative Imaginations); title (Me & My Big Ideas)

Top 10-Album (Westrim); clip art (Dover Publications)

Wild Artist-Journal (Chameleon Books); letter stickers (Creative Imaginations)

Oriental Clip-(Target)

Easter Brunch-Cards, envelope (Paper Adventures); image (Me & My Big Ideas); bands (Target)

Happy Birthday-Album (Kolo); word stamp (Paper Candy); sticker (Colorbök); rhinestone (Westrim)

Thanks-Album (Mirage Paper Company); letter stickers (Doodlebug Design)

Class of '89-Album (Boku Books); stickers (Hallmark); alphabet rub-ons (Creative Imaginations)

A Star Is Born-Tags (Creative Imaginations)

Movie Tickets-Paper (Paper Loft); die cut (EK Success); fibers (Making Memories)

Toby's Birthday-Paper (Paper Loft); letter stamps (Hero Arts)

'62 Corvair-Tag album (DMD); paper, rub-ons, letter stickers (Creative Imaginations); metal tags (Scrap Ease)

My Job-Letter stickers (All My Memories)

Containers-Green H box (Kolo); heart stickers (Creative Imaginations); cigar box, moon box, lunchbox (found, source unknown)

Pages 14-15, Many Mini Options!

Sun-Album (DMD); stamp (Rubber Stampede)

Sweet-Tags (Gartner Studios); word sticker (Creative Imaginations); chain (Westrim); charm (Blue Moon Beads)

Enjoy-Tiny file folders (EK Success); girl and heart die-cuts (Meri Meri); word (All My Memories); clips (Scrapworks)

Christmas Book-Album (Canson); paper (Frances Meyer, Reminiscence Papers); border stickers (Mrs. Grossman's); fibers (Scrapworks); buttons (Doodlebug Design)

Woman Box-Box (source unknown); paper (DMD); glitter (Ranger); flower (vintage)

School Days-Index cards (Target); image (Design Originals); paper (Karen Foster Design); letter stickers (Mrs. Grossman's, Wordsworth); binding discs (Rollabind); stamp (Rubber Stampede)

Dad-Business card holder (source unknown); letter stickers (Karen Foster Design)

Helen-Tags (source unknown); stamps (Hampton Art Stamps); fibers (Rubba Dub Dub); paper (Carolee's Creations); beads (Blue Moon Beads)

The Nursery-Die cut (Meri Meri); letter stickers (Creative Imaginations); stamp (Rubber Stampede)

Girls Will Be Girls-Album (Lady Jayne); paper (Scrapbook Wizard, Westrim); word sticker (Sassafras Lass)

A Day-Card (Meri Meri); word sticker (Sassafras Lass); rhinestones (Me & My Big Ideas)

Once Upon a Time-Diary (source unknown); fabric words, images, leaves (ARTchix Studio)

Frame-Frame (PTI Group); paper (Creative Imaginations)

Candleholder-Candleholder (source unknown); paper (Westrim); prism paper (Grafix); stickers (Frances Meyer)

25 Years-Paper (Magenta); acrylic square (Creative Imaginations); charm (Boutique Trims)

Mom-Container (Tidy Crafts); paper (Paper Adventures); stickers (Wordsworth); flowers (vintage)

Travel Tin-Tin (ARTchix Studio); globe (Magic Scraps)

Pages 20-21, Celebrate Companions
Laura-Paper (DMD, Karen Foster Design); stamps and ink (Clearsnap); wording (vintage); flower stickers (Paper House Productions); glitter (Art Institute Glitter); sheet adhesive (Therm O Web)

Friends-Paper (Creative Imaginations, Masterpiece Studios); stamp (Paper Candy); rub-on words (Scrap Ease); charm, glitter (Magic Scraps); sheet adhesive (Therm O Web)

My Friends-Journal (source unknown); paper (Creative Imaginations, KI Memories, Scrapbook Wizard); letter stickers (KI Memories); glitter (Magic Scraps); button (source unknown)

Props-Charms (Boutique Trims)

Pages 22-23, Praise Parents
Mom-Cloth, charm (vintage); paper (Creative Imaginations, KI Memories, Paper Loft, Paper Love Designs, Rocky Mountain Scrapbook Co.); shoes stamp (Hampton Art Stamps); flower stamp, kiss stamp (Rubber Stampede); spiral stamp (Clearsnap); letter stickers (Paper Loft); square stickers (Mrs. Grossman's)

Daddy, Dad, Father, Papa-Tags (Paper Loft); paper (Paper Love Designs); word tiles (Doodlebug Design); border and circle stickers (Mrs. Grossman's); rivet stickers (Stampendous!); fibers (Rubba Dub Dub); charm (vintage); copper pen (Ranger)

#1 Dad-Slide mounts (Loersch); faux fur (Grafix); charm (found)

Props-Images (ARTchix Studio); charms (Boutique Trims)

Pages 24-25, Herald Heritage
Necklace-Frame (ARTchix Studio); paper (DMD); beads (Blue Moon Beads); rhinestones, illusion cord (Westrim); paper glaze (Duncan); sheet adhesive (Therm O Web)

Pin With Charm-Frame (source unknown); paper (DMD); charm (Blue Moon Beads); rhinestones (Mrs. Grossman's)

Pin With Micro Beads-Frame (source unknown); paper (Creative Imaginations, Paper Adventures)

Earrings-Metal tags, paper (source un-

known); hooks (Blue Moon Beads); jump rings (Westrim); metal heart and star (Limited Edition Rubberstamps); rhinestones (Me & My Big Ideas)

Bracelet-Bracelet (ARTchix Studio); paper (Karen Foster Design); clear epoxy stickers (Making Memories)

Props-Buttons (JHB International)

Pages 26-27, Protect Pets
My Pets-Paper (DMD, Doodlebug Design); clip art (Dover Publications); cover image (found); letter tiles (Doodlebug Design); stickers (Gartner Studios); clips, staples (Office Depot)

Meow-Notecards (Mara-Mi); paper (Frances Meyer); vellum (source unknown); rolling stamp (Clearsnap); letter stickers (Wordsworth); beads (JewelCraft); rhinestones (Westrim), clips (Target)

Lulu-Notecards (Gartner Studios); letter stickers (Me & My Big Ideas); button (JHB International); clips (Target)

Props-Clips (Making Memories); charms (Boutique Trims, JHB International)

Pages 28-29, Log Life
My Life-CD sleeves (Target); paper (Doodlebug Design, KI Memories); # stamps (Hero Arts); letter and word stickers (Creative Imaginations, Karen Foster Design, Me & My Big Ideas, Scrapworks, Wordsworth); alphabet template (C-Thru Ruler); purse die cut (Meri Meri); stickers (Frances Meyer, Mrs. Grossman's); charms (ARTchix Studio, Blue Moon Beads, Boutique Trims, found, vintage); clips, jump rings (Westrim); glitter writer (Duncan)

Life Is Good-Label (Me & My Big Ideas); fabric words (ARTchix Studio); flower punch (EK Success)

Pages 30-31, Magnetize Memories
Carlie-Square (Provo Craft); paper (Bisous); letter tiles (Limited Edition Rubberstamps); stickers (Autumn Leaves); buttons (Doodlebug Design)

Love-Heart (Provo Craft); paper (Karen Foster Design, Me & My Big Ideas); flower (Westrim)

Let's Eat-Rectangle (Lara's Crafts); paper (Karen Foster Design, Scrapbook Wizard); rhinestones (Me & My Big Ideas); charms (source unknown)

Max-House (Provo Craft); paper (DMD, Karen Foster Design); letter stamps (Paper Candy); button (vintage)

Star-Star (Provo Craft); paper (DMD); rhinestones (Westrim)

Summertime-Circle (source unknown); paper (Bisous); letter stickers (Scrapbook Wizard); die cut (Cropper Hopper); fibers (Rubba Dub Dub)

Baby-Circle (Lara's Crafts); paper (Scrapbook Wizard)

Flowers-Wooden shapes (Forster); paper (KI Memories); stickers (Stampendous!)

Wrapped Magnets-Paint chips (found); images (Stampa Rosa); cellophane (DMD); transparency (Magic Scraps);

rhinestones, ribbon (Me & My Big Ideas)

Props-Wooden shapes (Lara's Crafts, Provo Craft)

Pages 32-33, Remember Reunions
Family Reunion-Cards (DMD); paper (DMD, Me & My Big Ideas, Paper Loft); images (found); cloth (source unknown); large cherry stamp (Duncan), small cherry stamp (Clearsnap); label stamp (Rubber Stampede); bands (circo); ribbon (ARTchix Studio); floss (DMC); embossing powders (Ranger)

A Fun Time-Card (Gartner Studios); paper (Creative Imaginations); stamp (River City Rubber Works); rhinestones (Westrim); bands (Target)

Props-Bands (Circo, Target); caps (Collage Joy)

Pages 34-35, Document Days
Sunday-Stencils (Hunt); paper (Paper Loft); images (found); dog stamp (The Stamp Pad Co.); border stickers (Mrs. Grossman's)

A Day in the Life-Envelopes (Gartner Studios); paper (Karen Foster Design, Magic Scraps, NRN Designs); epoxy stickers (EK Success); flower stickers (Frances Meyer); eyelet stickers (Stampendous!); bead chain (Magic Scraps)

Life's a Beach-Tags (Paper Loft); paper (Paper Adventures); stamp (River City Rubber Works); rub-on letters (ChartPak); eyelets (Westrim); charms, shells (found, vintage)

A Day at the Zoo-Paper (DMD, Karen Foster Design); animal stamps (All Night Media), letter stamps (Hero Arts); embossing powder (Stampendous!)

Girls' Night Out-Vinyl pockets (Better Office Products); paper, word sticker (Sassafras Lass); heart stamp, foil, star stickers (Stampendous!); epoxy stickers (EK Success); safety pins (Westrim)

Dad, Mom, Brother, Sister-Notepads (Bridgeport); paper (Magic Scraps); letter stickers (All My Memories, Scrapbook Wizard)

Pages 38-39, Frame Flowers
My Garden-Frames (Westrim); transparency (Magic Scraps); sticker square (Mrs. Grossman's); charm (vintage); mounting squares (3L)

Sunflowers-Frames (Cropper Hopper); sticker square (Mrs. Grossman's); letters, bead, charms (found, vintage)

Bouquet-Frames (K & Company); transparency (Magic Scraps); clip art pattern (source unknown); hinges (vintage), ink (Clearsnap)

Props-Charms (Boutique Trims)

Pages 40-41, Request RSVPs
Backyard BBQ-Paper (Four Peas); stickers (Gartner Studios); swizzle stick (Accoutrements)
Pajama Party-Paper (Four Peas, Sassafras Lass); letter stickers (Scrapbook Wizard); stickers (Karen Foster Design); label (Gartner Studios); swizzle stick (Accoutrements)
9/13/02-Paper (Esselte); rub-on letters (ChartPak); party pick (Amscan)
Props-Pick (Amscan); sticks (Accoutrements)

Pages 42-43, Instill Inspiration
The Sky Is the Limit-Box (found); word stickers (Wordsworth); charm (Boutique Trims); fibers (Magic Scraps)
Green Album-Album (Kolo); word stickers (Wordsworth); epoxy sticker (Creative Imaginations)
30 Reasons-Paint chips, lettering (found); paper (KI Memories)
Smile-Box (The Container Store); word tile (KI Memories)
Celebrate Life-Cloth label (Me & My Big Ideas)
Props-Labels (Me & My Big Ideas); metal words (Making Memories)

Pages 44-45, Visit Vacations
Hawaii-Coasters (ORE); textured paper (Magic Scraps); wrapping paper images (source unknown); stamps (Paper Candy); stickers (Creative Imaginations); charm (Boutique trims)
Mexico-Coasters (ORE); stickers (EK Success); images, charms, fibers (found, vintage); rhinestones (Me & My Big Ideas); glitter writer (Ranger)
Road Trip-Coasters (source unknown); metallic paper, compass nailhead (Magic Scraps); letter stickers (Karen Foster Design); charm (Boutique Trims); brads (Doodlebug Design)
Milk Caps-(Collage Joy); paper (Memories Forever)
Tiki-Coaster (Accoutrements); album (The Container Store)
Steps-Coasters (Cost Plus)
Props-Buttons and charms (Accoutrements, JHB International, Magic Scraps)

Pages 46-47, Record Romance
Lucky in Love-Shadow box (EK Success); paper (KI Memories); images (Design Originals); letters (found); charms (ARTchix Studio)
Cecile Et Marcel-Box (The Container Store); paper (Paper Love Designs); letter stamps (Hero Arts); charms (Boutique Trims); buttons (JHB International); ribbon (Robin's Nest)
E and T-Tin (Provo Craft); transparency (Magic Scraps); frame (Westrim); epoxy stickers (EK Success); letters, charms (vintage)

Andrew and Laura-Box (The Container Store); stamps (JudiKins, Rubber Stampede); jewelry and leaves (vintage)
Photo Booth-Box (source unknown); transparency (Magic Scraps)
Las Vegas Penny-Box (The Container Store); paper (DMD); charms (ARTchix Studio)
Props-Charms (Boutique Trims)

Pages 48-49, Lavish Luck
Good Luck-Album (Graeham Owens); images, paper charms (ARTchix Studio); plastic lens (Scrapworks); cloth label (Me & My Big Ideas); charm (Boutique Trims); rhinestones (Mrs. Grossman's); glitter (Magic Scraps)
Rachel And Alex-Paper (Creative Imaginations); plastic lens (Scrapworks); fortune stickers (Me & My Big Ideas); micro beads (Magic Scraps); ribbon (Robin's Nest)
Lucky 7-Box, bottle cap, dice, fortunes (found); paper (KI Memories); rhinestones (Beadery); beads (JewelCraft)
Props-Charm (Boutique Trims)

Pages 50-51, Fashion Favors
Carol And Frank-Cellophane bag (source unknown); coins (Cost Plus); mylar shred (Magic Scraps)
Amy & John-Cellophane bag (source unknown); clip art (Dover Publications); ribbon (The Robin's Nest)
Lordy, Lordy-Cellophane bag (source unknown)
Five-Cellophane (DMD); prism paper (Grafix); letter stickers (Frances Meyer)
Baby Shower-Cellophane (DMD); tag (American Tag)
Kindred Spirits-Cloth bag (Creative Imaginations); paper (DMD); word sticker (Wordsworth); pin, bead, charm (vintage)
Las Vegas-Cellophane (DMD); rhinestones (Westrim); favors, fillers (Accoutrements, found, vintage)

Pages 52-53, Archive Autographs
Best Wishes-Paper (KI Memories); die cuts (Meri Meri); rub-on letters (ChartPak); photo corners (Kolo); ribbon (Making Memories)
Autographs-Paper (Paper Loft); images (found); ticket stub (EK Success); letters (ARTchix Studio); typewriter key (Foofala)
Bon Voyage-Album (Kolo); paper (Paper Love Designs); rub-on letters, epoxy sticker (Creative Imaginations); gold tape (Grafix)
Steps-Paper (Sassafras Lass)

Pages 56-57, Save Sonograms
Baby Names-Paper, die cuts (KI Memories); stamp (River City Rubber Works); acrylic square (Creative Imaginations); letter stickers (Scrapbook Wizard); number stickers (Boxer Scrapbook Productions); floss (Scrapworks); silver glaze (Rubber Stampede)
Secret Words-Paper (KI Memories); ? sticker (Doodlebug Design); glass bead (Magic Scraps)

Pages 58-59, Track Time
9 Months-Album (DMD); wooden rectangle (Provo Craft); paper (DMD, Me & My Big Ideas); letter stickers (Wordsworth); letter tiles (Doodlebug Design); word labels (Dymo); stickers (EK Success); flowers (vintage); ribbon (Me & My Big Ideas, Scrapbook Wizard); nailheads (Scrapworks); paint (Plaid); ink (Clearsnap)
Year One-Album (Canson); wooden circles (Lara's Crafts); paper (Karen Foster Design); letter stamps (Hero Arts); letter stencil (Magic Scraps); labels (Foofala); paper ribbon (DMD); paint (Plaid)
Milo-Album (Graeham Owens); wooden squares (Forster); stamps (Rubber Stampede); letter stencil (C-Thru Ruler); paint (Delta)
Props-Image and charm (ARTchix Studio)

Pages 60-61, Announce Arrivals
Angelina Rose-Transparency (Magic Scraps); letter stamps (Close To My Heart, Hero Arts); paint (Plaid)
It's A Boy-Transparencies (Magic Scraps); paper (KI Memories); die cut (Meri Meri); jump ring (Westrim)
Newborn-Transparency (Magic Scraps); clip art pattern (source unknown); paper (Creative Imaginations); staples (Office Depot)

Pages 62-63, Collect Characters
Whattabunch of Characters-Notebook (Igo Productions Inc.); paper (Paper Fever); frame, stamp (Clearsnap); letter stickers (KI Memories); word labels (Dymo); sticker (EK Success); star token (Doodlebug Design)
Meeting Disney-Address book (source unknown); paper (Scrapbook Wizard); prism paper (Grafix); frame (Clearsnap); letter tiles (Doodlebug Design); stickers (EK Success)
Steps-Frame (Clearsnap); flowers (vintage); permanent marker (Sanford)

Pages 64-65, Maintain Mementos
Happy Birthday-Album (source unknown); paper (Scrapbook Wizard); gift wrap (American Greetings); metallic paper (Magic Scraps); die cut (Meri Meri); stamp (Rubber Stampede)
Snips and Snails-Album (source unknown); paper (Frances Meyer, Making Memories); baby clothes (Land's End, Zutano)
Teddy-Album (source unknown); paper (Paper Loft); tickets (Collage Joy); letter stickers (KI Memories); stickers (Creative Imaginations, EK Success); photo corners (Kolo)
Props-Chick die-cut (Meri Meri)

Pages 66-67, Preserve Portraits
Grade School-Matchbox (DMD); paper (KI Memories); number stickers (Doodlebug Design); toys, charms (found, vintage); rhinestones (Westrim); beads (Blue Moon Beads); glaze (Ranger)
Katie-Matchbox and paper (DMD); metal-

lic paper (Me & My Big Ideas); plastic lens (Scrapworks); stamps (Just For Fun Rubber Stamps); image, charms (vintage); beads (source unknown); glaze (Ranger)
Friends-Matchbox (found); paper (KI Memories); letter beads (Westrim); buttons Karen Foster Design, vintage)
Steps-Matchbox (DMD); paper (Me & My Big Ideas)

Pages 68-69, Give Games
Puzzle Cubes-Wooden cubes (Michaels); paper (Design Originals, Me & My Big Ideas); letter stickers (Paper Loft); decoupage medium (Plaid)
Memory Game-Lids (found); paper (Bisous, Stampin' Up!); letter stickers (Creative Imaginations); decoupage medium (Plaid)

Pages 72-73, Capture Collections
Salt & Pepper Shakers-Fabric (Makings); iron-on vinyl, sheet adhesive (Therm O web); letters (found); word labels (Dymo); cord (source unknown)
Valentines-Memorabilia pockets (Therm O Web); fabric (Junkitz, Makings); stickers (Karen Foster Design); heart (Meri Meri); floss (DMC); buttons (source unknown)
Fruit Plaques-Oilcloth (source unknown); jump rings (Westrim)

Pages 74-75, Keep Keys
Ronnie and Pam-Key chain (Lucky Line Products); paper (Hallmark); frame (Me & My Big Ideas); stickers (Frances Meyer)
Husband-Laminate chip (found); paper (KI Memories); frame (All My Memories)
Family-Key chain (Hillman); letter stickers (KI Memories); letter beads (Westrim); bead chain (Magic Scraps)
My Boy-Key chain (source unknown); paper (Scrapbook Wizard); word sticker (Sassafras Lass)
Friend-Tags (Magic Scraps); word tile (KI Memories)
Play-Tag (Magic Scraps); word sticker (Creative Imaginations); sticker (Sandylion); bead chain (Westrim); rhinestones (Me & My Big Ideas)
Lisa-Frame (Westrim); metallic paper (Magic Scraps)
Heritage-Tags (Scrap Ease); stickers (Me & My Big Ideas); metal shapes (Limited Editon Rubber Stamps); charm (Boutique Trims)

Pages 76-77, Shake Snow
Winter Wonderland-Dome (Summit Products); prism paper (Grafix); images (vintage); paper snowflakes (EK Success); snowman and snowflake button (JHB International); dimensional paint (Stampendous!); rhinestones (Westrim)
Home Is Where the Heart Is-Dome (Summit Products); paper, images (DMD, Me & My Big Ideas); cloth label (Me & My Big Ideas); word labels (Dymo); sticker (Stampendous!); metal shapes (Limited Edition Rubberstamps); charm (Boutique Trims); heart button (JHB International); bead,

rhinestones (Westrim)
Home Sweet Home-Dome (East West Distribution Co.); letter beads, flower (Westrim); butterfly (found)
Tiki Lounge-Dome (Summit Products); sticker (Sassafras Lass); party pick (Amscan); metal shapes (Limited Edition Rubberstamps); flamingo (found)
There's No Place Like Home-Dome (source unknown); stickers (Stampendous!); button (JHB International); micro beads (Magic Scraps)
Props-Snowflake buttons (Blumenthal Lansing Co.); angel and sled buttons (source unknown)

Pages 78-79, Present Pumpkins
Halloween Pumpkins-Paper (Creative Imaginations); images (Paper Love Designs); stamps (Rubber Stampede); letter stickers, brads (All My Memories); punch (EK Success); ink (Clearsnap)
Happy Halloween-Stamps (Paper Candy); rolling stamps, ink (Clearsnap); brads (Keeping Memories Alive)
Props-Buttons (Doodlebug Design)

Pages 80-81, Give Gratitude
Rob-Acrylic frames (Westrim); paper (Paper Loft); letter stickers (Creative Imaginations); brads (Karen Foster Design); tape (Venture tape)
Linda-Acrylic frames (Westrim); paper (DMD); brads (Karen Foster Design); tape (Venture Tape)
Lisa-Acrylic squares (Magenta); tape (Venture tape)
Mollie-Acrylic squares (Magenta); paper, image (Paper Love Designs); letter stamps (Hero Arts); tape (Venture tape)
Leaves-Acrylic squares (Magenta); paper (Paper Loft); die cuts (EK Success)
Give Thanks-Acrylic squares (Magenta); paper (Paper Love Designs); button (vintage); tape (Venture tape)
Props-Leaf die cuts (EK Success)

Pages 82-83, Treasure Traditions
Happy Holidays-Box (source unknown); paper (Creative Imaginations); stamps (Clearsnap, Hero Arts, JudiKins, Wordsworth); word stamp (Rubber Stampede); dimensional paint (Ranger); ribbon (Making Memories); shred (DMD)
Charmed Life-Tin (The Container Store); stamps (Just For Fun Rubber Stamps, Paper Candy, Rubber Stampede); letter stamps (Hero Arts); charms (Boutique Trims, vintage)
Fragile-Box (source unknown); paper (Paper Love Designs); stickers (Me & My Big Ideas); label (vintage); tag (Stampendous!); fibers (Scrapworks)
Our Family Traditions-Tin (found); paper (Paper Loft); transparency image (Limited Edition Rubberstamps); tiny image (ARTchix Studio); stamp, letter stickers (Stampendous!); definition (Foofala)
Hanukkah-Tin (The Container Store); prism paper (Emagination Crafts); die cut (Meri

Meri); dimensional sticker (Magenta)
Lullabies-Tin (The Container Store); stamp (Limited Edition Rubberstamps); letter template (Magic Scraps); moon (Boutique Trims); stars (found)
Heart-Tin (vintage); paper (DMD); glass bead (Magic Scraps); stamp (Hero Arts)
Props-Die cuts (Meri Meri); buttons (JHB International); game pieces (Westrim Crafts)

Pages 84-85, Create Countdowns
The 12 Days of X-mas-Album (Kolo); scratch paper (Hampton Art Stamps); border stickers (Mrs. Grossman's); stamps (Hampton Art Stamps, Magenta); tag (Gartner Studios)
Happy New Year-Card (Gartner Studios); scratch Paper (Hampton Art Stamps); paper (source unknown); blank postage (Stampendous!); images (DMD); stamps (Clearsnap, Just For Fun Rubber Stamps); letter stamps (Hero Arts, Paper Candy); charm (Boutique Trims)
Happy Hanukkah-Card (DMD); scratch paper (Hampton Art Stamps); paper (Paper Loft); die cuts (EK Success); letters (Foofala); number stamps (Stamp Craft)
Your Secret Santa Is-Library pocket (Queen-Of-Tarts); scratch paper (Hampton Art Stamps); paper (Frances Meyer); die cut (Meri Meri); stamps (Clearsnap); word stamp (Paper Candy); letter stickers (Wordsworth); eyelets (ScrapArts); ribbon (source unknown); dimensional paint (Ranger); punch (EK Success)

Pages 86-87, Foretell Futures
New Year's Resolutions 2004-Bingo cards (Karen Foster Design); paper, tag (Scrapbook Wizard); tags (Gartner Studios); letter stamps (Stamp Craft); fibers (Magic Scraps); glitter paint (DecoArt); binding punch, discs (Rollabind)
Predictions 2005-Loteria cards (Gallo); silver paper (Me & My Big Ideas); color block (Scrapbook Wizard); rolling stamp (Clearsnap); frame (Scrap Ease); number stickers (Karen Foster Design); plastic lens (Scrapworks); rhinestones (Magic Scraps); binding punch, discs (Rollabind)
Camille-Cards (vintage); binding punch, discs (Rollabind)
Happy New Year-Binding punch and discs (Rollabind)
Props-Game pieces (Westrim)

Resource Guide

3L Corp.
(800) 828-3130
www.scrapbook-adhesives.com

All My Memories
(888) 553-1998
www.allmymemories.com

All Night Media® (see Plaid Enterprises)

Amscan, Inc.
(800) 444-8887
www.amscan.com

Archie McPhee® & Company
(425) 349-3009
www.mcphee.com

ARTchix Studio™
(250) 370-9885
www.artchixstudio.com

Better Office Products®
(818) 598-0005
www.betteroffice.com

Blue Moon Beads
(800) 377-6715
www.bluemoonbeads.com

Boku Books®
(888) 924-BOKU
www.bokubooks.com

Boutique Trims, Inc.
(248) 437-2017
www.boutiquetrims.com

Canson, Inc.®
(800) 628-9283
www.canson-us.com

ChartPak
(800) 628-1910
www.chartpak.com

Clearsnap, Inc.
(800) 448-4862
www.clearsnap.com

Club Scrap™
(888) 634-9100
www.clubscrap.com

Collage Joy
www.collagejoy.com

Container Store, The
(888) 266-8246
www.thecontainerstore.com

Cost Plus World Market
(510) 893-7300
www.costpluscom

Creative Imaginations
(800) 942-6487
www.cigift.com

C-Thru® Ruler Company, The
(800) 243-8419
www.cthruruler.com

Design Originals
(800) 877-7820
www.d-originals.com

DMD Industries, Inc.
(800) 805-9890
www.dmdind.com

Doodlebug Design, Inc.™
(801) 952-0555
www.doodlebugdesigninc.com

Dover Publications, Inc.
(800) 223-3130
www.doverpublications.com

Dymo
www.dymo.com

EK Success™
(800) 524-1349
www.eksuccess.com

Emagination Crafts, Inc.
(866) 238-9770
www.emaginationcrafts.com

Fiskars, Inc.
(800) 950-0203
www.fiskars.com

Font Diner
www.fontdiner.com

Forster® Craft Division/Alltrista
Consumer Products
(800) 777-7942
www.diamondbrands.com

Four Peas
(949) 307-3827
www.fourpeas.net

Frances Meyer
(413) 584-5446
www.francesmeyer.com

Gartner Studios, Inc.
www.uprint.com

Glue Dots® International
(888) 688-7131
www.gluedots.com

Graeham Owens
(800) 805-0012
www.graehamowens.com

Grafix®
(800) 447-2349
www.grafixarts.com

Hampton Art Stamps, Inc.
(800) 229-1019
www.hamptonart.com

Hero Arts® Rubber Stamps, Inc.
(800) 822-4376
www.heroarts.com

JewelCraft, LLC
(201) 223-0804
www.jewelcraft.biz

JHB International, Inc
(303) 751-8100
www.buttons.com

JudiKins
(310) 515-1115
www.judikins.com

Just For Fun® Rubber Stamps
(727) 938-9898
www.jffstamps.com

Karen Foster Design
(801) 451-9779
www.karenfosterdesign.com

KI Memories
(469) 633-9665
www.kimemories.com

Kolo®, LLC
(888) 636-5656
www.kolo.com

Lady Jayne, Ltd.
(800) 293-3564
www.ladyjayne.com

Land's End, Inc.
(800) 332-0103
www.landsend.com

Lara's Crafts
(800) 232-5272
www.larascrafts.com

Limited Edition Rubberstamps
(650) 594-4242
www.limitededitionrs.com

Lucky Line Products, Inc.
(800) 654-6409
www.luckyline.com

Magenta Rubber Stamps
(800) 565-5254
www.magentastyle.com

Magic Scraps™
(972) 385-1838
www.magicscraps.com

Making Memories
(800) 286-5263
www.makingmemories.com

me & my BiG ideas®
(949) 583-2065
www.meandmybigideas.com

Meri Meri
www.merimeri.com

Mrs. Grossman's Paper Company
(800) 429-4549
www.mrsgrossmans.com

Office Depot
www.officedepot.com

Paper Adventures®
(800) 727-0699
www.paperadventures.com

Paper Candy
www.papercandy.com

Paper Fever, Inc.
(800) 477-0902
www.paperfever.com

Paper House Productions
(800) 255-7316
www.paperhouseproductions.com

Paper Loft, The
(866) 254-1961
www.paperloft.com

Paper Love Designs
(510) 841-1088
www.paperlovedesigns.com

Plaid Enterprises, Inc.
(800) 842-4197
www.plaidonline.com

Provo Craft®
(888) 577-3545
www.provocraft.com

Queen of Tarts Stamps
www.queen-of-tarts.com

Ranger Industries, Inc.
(800) 244-2211
www.rangerink.com

Reminiscence Papers
(503) 246-9681
www.reminiscencepapers.com

Rollabind, LLC
(800) 438-3542
www.rollabind.com

Rubber Stampede
(800) 423-4135
www.deltacrafts.com

Sassafras Lass
(801) 269-1331
www.sassafraslass.com

Scrapbook Wizard™, The
(435) 752-7555
www.scrapbookwizard.com

Scrap Ease®
(800) 272-3874
www.whatsnewltd.com

Scrapworks™, LLC
(801) 363-1010
www.scrapworks.com

Stampendous!®
(800) 869-0474
www.stampendous.com

Target
www.target.com

Therm O Web, Inc.
(800) 323-0799
www.thermoweb.com

Tidy Crafts
(208) 523-2565
www.tidycrafts.com

Venture Tape
(800) 343-1076
www.venturetape.com

Westrim® Crafts
(800) 727-2727
www.westrimcrafts.com

Wordsworth
(719) 282-3495
www.wordsworthstamps.com

Zutano®
www.zutano.com

Patterns

Use these helpful patterns to create projects featured on the pages noted. Photocopy and enlarge patterns as desired.

Announce Arrivals

Pages 60-61

Log Life

Pages 28-29

Treasure Traditions

Pages 82-83

Bio

Pamela Frye Hauer's talents and professional experience in photography, graphic design, gift design and special-event planning prepared her for her current career in the world of scrapbooking and memory crafts. Once a member of the *Memory Makers* staff, Pamela transitioned from full-time employment into a freelance career where she now enjoys balancing her time as a parent with authoring books for the books division. Pamela also contributes her work to other industry publications and Web sites and lends her consultation to several scrapbook product manufacturers. Additionally, Pamela creates artwork for gifts, for sale and for trade with other artists. She lives in Denver, Colorado, with her family and pets and her ever-expanding collection of photos and mementos.

Index